*The Cambridge Introduction to*
## George Orwell

Arguably the most influential political writer of the twentieth century, George Orwell remains a crucial voice for our times. Known worldwide for his two bestselling masterpieces – *Nineteen Eighty-Four*, a gripping portrait of a dystopian future, and *Animal Farm*, a brilliant satire on the Russian Revolution – Orwell has been revered as an essayist, journalist, and literary-political intellectual, and his works have exerted a powerful international impact in the post-World War II era. The *Cambridge Introduction* examines Orwell's life, work, and legacy, addressing his towering achievement and his ongoing appeal. Combining biographical detail with close analysis of his writings, the book considers the various genres in which Orwell wrote: realistic novel, essay, reportage, fable, and anti-utopia. Written for both new and for already well-informed readers of Orwell's work, the present study concludes with an extended reflection on why George Orwell has enjoyed a literary afterlife unprecedented among modern authors in any language.

JOHN RODDEN has taught at the University of Virginia and the University of Texas at Austin. He is currently Visiting Professor in the Department of Foreign Languages at Tunghai University, Taiwan. He has published nine books on Orwell, including *The Cambridge Companion to George Orwell* (2007). He is presently working on a co-edited volume, *Orwell: Orienting Asian Perspectives*, with Henk Vynckier, Professor at Tunghai University.

JOHN ROSSI is Professor Emeritus of History at La Salle University, Philadelphia. Along with his interest in George Orwell, he has also written extensively about major topics in British history, particularly the life and times of Winston Churchill.

The Cambridge Introduction to
# George Orwell

JOHN RODDEN

and

JOHN ROSSI

CAMBRIDGE
UNIVERSITY PRESS

CAMBRIDGE UNIVERSITY PRESS
Cambridge, New York, Melbourne, Madrid, Cape Town,
Singapore, São Paulo, Delhi, Mexico City

Cambridge University Press
The Edinburgh Building, Cambridge CB2 8RU, UK

Published in the United States of America by Cambridge University Press, New York

www.cambridge.org
Information on this title: www.cambridge.org/9780521132558

First published 2012

Printed in the United Kingdom at the University Press, Cambridge

*A catalogue record for this publication is available from the British Library*

*Library of Congress Cataloguing in Publication data*
Rodden, John.
The Cambridge introduction to George Orwell / John Rodden, John Rossi.
   pages   cm
ISBN 978-0-521-76923-5 (hardback)
1. Orwell, George, 1903–1950.   I. Rossi, John, 1936–   II. Title.
PR6029.R8Z7752   2012
828′.91209–dc23
[B]

2012000082

ISBN 978-0-521-76923-5 Hardback
ISBN 978-0-521-13255-8 Paperback

To Peter Davison
Friend, colleague, and editor *extraordinaire*

# Contents

# Preface

Since his death in January 1950 at the age of forty-six, George Orwell's critical and popular reputation has ascended and spread wings. Three major biographies were published during the last decade and Orwell's papers have been edited in twenty volumes by the British scholar Peter Davison. Special studies dealing with Orwell's career and writings appear annually.

Recognized internationally chiefly for his last two masterpieces – *Animal Farm* (1945), his brilliant satire on the Russian Revolution, and *Nineteen Eighty-Four* (1949), his gripping dystopian portrait of the future – Orwell's other body of writing also enjoys an appreciative audience today.

Our study examines the reasons for Orwell's ongoing appeal. Combining biography with an analysis of his writings, we focus on the main literary genres in which Orwell wrote: his traditional novels, his essays, and his documentary journalism.

In the 1930s, Orwell struggled to write realistic fiction. Two of his novels in particular, *Burmese Days* and *Coming Up for Air*, exhibit skillfully developed characters and descriptive passages even as they reveal the limitations of his fictional imagination.

Orwell's essays are among his best writing. He took a format that was being swamped by belles-lettres and breathed new life into it. In his greatest essays – "A Hanging," "Shooting an Elephant," and "Politics and the English Language" – Orwell discovered settings and subject matters that suited the prose style that he had developed: clear, direct, pared of artifice. By writing about topics avoided by serious authors (comic postcards, murder mysteries, and other mundane everyday things), Orwell also helped create the genre of popular cultural studies.

"Good prose," he once wrote, "is like a windowpane, it hides nothing." Orwell's conversational prose influenced a generation of writers and critics.

We also believe that in his documentary journalism, such as *The Road to Wigan Pier* and *Homage to Catalonia*, Orwell pioneered the emerging role of serious investigative journalist at its best.

Finally, Orwell created a persona that has won the admiration and trust of generations of Western intellectuals. It is the image of the honest man who recognizes his own flaws. This persona turned Orwell in the decades following his premature death into a mythic figure who has spawned imitators in pursuit of his mantle. Our study concludes with an analysis of the powerful myth of "St. George Orwell."

An original writer and thinker who lived a life of political commitment and social action, George Orwell warrants literary and public attention today.

## Acknowledgments

It is both a pleasure and an honor to have the opportunity to present a cherished author of mine to a new generation of readers in this *Cambridge Introduction to George Orwell*. This study marks my eighth book devoted to Orwell. It is a surprising and wondrous pleasure for me that I continue to learn from his rich and multifaceted work, to discover fresh perspectives about his complicated life and checkered legacy, and above all to gain unexpected insights about these matters from fellow students of his writings.

My debts to both colleagues and friends for sharing their perceptions about Orwell are too many to enumerate here. But let me at least acknowledge the deepest one: to my co-author, John P. Rossi, Professor Emeritus of History at La Salle University in Philadelphia. I have known Jack for nearly four decades, ever since my undergraduate days, and it has been a highlight of my last decade to collaborate with him on several essays about British and American intellectuals, including Orwell. *The Cambridge Introduction to George Orwell* marks our most ambitious joint undertaking, and it has proven yet again to be an intellectually edifying and personally fulfilling experience to learn from Jack anew. These chapters represent a fully cooperative venture – an act of scholarly "teamwork" as intellectual fraternity – and it has been wonderfully enlightening to share our drafts and our doubts in the course of its composition. For me, the most gratifying intellectual outcome of our miniature socialist collective is that I have simply grown further in my respect for Orwell's literary talents, particularly because I do not consider him to be a naturally gifted writer. He had to work very hard at the craft, and he had to keep on working, in order to become the writer whom he hoped to be. I am enormously impressed with his dogged persistence and his towering achievement. More than ever, I consider him an exemplary figure, not only for aspiring writers and intellectuals, but for us all as citizens.

More than ever, he stands before me as my "intellectual big brother."

A final word about this book's dedication is in order. After conferring with Jack Rossi about our collaboration and our larger debts regarding this project, both of us wish to acknowledge an academic elder whose own editorial efforts have been indispensable for introducing Orwell to countless new students to his work: Peter Davison.

A scholar's scholar and the dean of Orwell editors, Peter is widely and deservedly known as the editor of the 20-volume *Complete Works of George Orwell*, along with an excellent short study of Orwell's literary and publishing career, among other books. These contributions to Orwell scholarship represent a labor of love that is rare in academic life today.

Quite apart from his scholarly achievements, however, Peter is an extraordinarily generous human being, who readily shares his encyclopedic knowledge of Orwelliana and his sovereign understanding of Orwell's life and times with anyone, whether a seasoned colleague or a fresh student of Orwell's work. I'm always astounded to read an essay on Orwell by Peter, because I usually feel that I am starting from scratch on the topic, as if I had never read any books or criticism about George Orwell before! This would be a humbling, if not humiliating, experience if it were not outweighed by the sheer intellectual excitement of following the argument of a patient teacher who soon infects me with his passion and enthusiasm for his topic. Without exception, Peter succeeds admirably every time. I know that Jack Rossi shares my conviction about all this, for we often say to each other: "We need to consult Davison's work on this point." Or I will simply tell Jack: "I need to ask Davison about that!"

For all these reasons and more, this book is for Peter.

John Rodden
December 2011

# Chronology

| | |
|---|---|
| 1903 | June 25. Eric Arthur Blair born in Motihari, Bengal. |
| 1904 | His mother returns to England with children and settles at Henley-on-Thames, Oxfordshire. |
| 1911–16 | Boards at St. Cyprian's private preparatory school at Eastbourne, Sussex. |
| 1917–21 | King's Scholar at Eton. Contributes to *The Election Times* and *College Days*. |
| 1922–27 | Serves with Indian Imperial Police in Burma. |
| 1927–28 | Tramping expeditions to East End of London. |
| 1928–29 | Lives in working-class district of Paris. Begins early drafts of *Down and Out in Paris and London* and *Burmese Days*. |
| 1930–31 | Returns to England. |
| 1932–33 | Teaches full-time at The Hawthorns, a small private school for boys, in Hayes, Middlesex. |
| 1933 | January 9. *Down and Out in Paris and London*, by "George Orwell," published by Victor Gollancz. |
| 1934 | October 25. *Burmese Days* published by Harper & Brothers, New York. |
| 1934–36 | October 1934 – January 1936. Part-time assistant at Booklover's Corner, 1 South End Road, Hampstead. |
| 1935 | March 11. *A Clergyman's Daughter* published by Gollancz. |
| 1936 | January 31 – March 30. In north of England for a book on unemployment conditions. |
| | April 20. Publication of *Keep the Aspidistra Flying* by Gollancz. |
| | June 9. Marries Eileen O'Shaughnessy at parish church in Wallington, Hertfordshire. |
| | September. "Shooting an Elephant," *New Writing*. |
| 1937 | January–June. Serves in Independent Labour Party contingent with militia of the POUM (Workers' Party of Marxist Unification) during the Spanish Civil War. |

March 8. *The Road to Wigan Pier* published by Gollancz in trade and Left Book Club editions.

May 20. Shot in throat by fascist sniper at Huesca.

June 23. Escapes with Eileen from Spain into France by train.

1938      April 25. *Homage to Catalonia*, having been refused by Gollancz, is published by Secker & Warburg.

1938–39    September 12 – March 26. In French Morocco (mainly at Marrakech); writes *Coming Up for Air*, published June 12 by Gollancz.

1940      March 11. *Inside the Whale and Other Essays* published by Gollancz.

1941      February 19. *The Lion and the Unicorn* published by Secker & Warburg (first of Searchlight Books series edited by Orwell and T. R. Fyvel).

1941–43    August 1941 – November 1943. Talks assistant, later talks producer, in Indian section of BBC's Eastern Service.

1943      November 24. Resigns from BBC and joins *Tribune* as Literary Editor (until 16 February 1945).

1945      March 29. Eileen Blair dies.

August 17. Publication of *Animal Farm* by Secker & Warburg in an edition of 4,500 copies.

1946      February 14. *Critical Essays* published by Secker & Warburg. *Animal Farm* published in USA.

1947      Writes "Such, Such Were the Joys"; completed about May 1948. First draft composed as early as 1946.

December 20. Patient in Hairmyres Hospital, East Kilbride (near Glasgow), suffering from tuberculosis; stays seven months.

1948      July 28. At Barnhill, Jura, for five months.

1949      January 6 – September 3. Patient in Cotswold Sanatorium Cranham, Gloucestershire, with serious case of tuberculosis.

June 8. Publication of *Nineteen Eighty-Four* by Secker & Warburg.

July. *Nineteen Eighty-Four* appears as Book-of-the-Month Club selection.

October 13. Marries Sonia Brownell.

1950      January 21. Dies of pulmonary tuberculosis, age forty-six.

January 26. Funeral at Christ Church, Albany Street, London. Buried, as Eric Arthur Blair, All Saints Cemetery, Sutton Courtenay, Berkshire.

# Introduction

Just days before he died in January 1950, George Orwell (born Eric Arthur Blair in 1903) penned in his notebook one of the epigrams that typified his stylistic talents: "After 50, everyone has the face he deserves."[1] Unfortunately, he never lived to fifty. He died at age forty-six, on the threshold of becoming "a famous author," his boyhood dream.[2] In the years since his death his fame has only grown.

Orwell's active literary life spanned less than two decades and yet he became perhaps the best-known English literary figure of the first half of the twentieth century. As he declared in "Why I Write" (1946), Orwell aspired to raise "political writing into an art."[3] In his greatest essays and his two final master-pieces, *Animal Farm* (1945) and *Nineteen Eighty-Four* (1949), he succeeded. In a poll done by Waterstone's, the English bookstore chain, readers ranked Orwell's last two works as the second and third most influential books of the twentieth century. (J. R. Tolkien's *Lord of the Rings* cycle came in first.)

Orwell initially wanted to write traditional fiction ("enormous naturalistic novels with unhappy endings"),[4] and in the 1930s he produced four such novels. They vary greatly in quality. *A Clergyman's Daughter* (1935) is subpar for him, though his *Burmese Days* (1934) and *Coming Up for Air* (1939) exhibit impressive novelistic skill – the former for its portrait of the British Empire in decline, the latter in its foreshadowing of World War II. All his novels were drawn from his own experiences. Although he tried to recreate them in his fiction, he lacked the imaginative gifts of a D. H. Lawrence or James Joyce. Orwell rejected many of his early writings in later years. But he did believe that *Coming Up for Air* could have been a considerable success if it had not been victimized by its publication date – it appeared in July 1939, just weeks before World War II broke out.

Orwell's finest writings, at least until *Animal Farm* (1945), are his essays and his documentaries, *The Road to Wigan Pier* (1937), which addresses the Depression in England's post-industrial north, and *Homage to Catalonia* (1938), which relates his experience in the Spanish Civil War. These works showed that Orwell had mastered a crisp, clear literary style, a mode of

1

composition purged of excess words, one that spoke directly to the reader. His deceptively simple prose was actually, according to biographer Michael Shelden, "the product of a highly sophisticated artistic process."[5] His "plain man" style would ultimately endear Orwell to generations of writers throughout the English-speaking world.

Orwell's essays and documentaries also show him to be a talented journalist. Later in his career he would edit the radical leftwing weekly, *Tribune*, and write a popular column that he called "As I Please." It was as idiosyncratic as its title and its author, dealing with anything that took Orwell's fancy: the names of English flowers, how to make a cup of tea, the decline of the English murder mystery, the habits of the common English toad, and so on. His friend Julian Symons noted that there was a deceptive child-like enjoyment of simple things in much of Orwell's writing. "Deceptive" is the operative word. Orwell had mastered the ability to say profound things in clear yet powerful prose. "Good prose," he wrote, "should be like a window pane";[6] it should hide nothing.

Orwell's style redirected the writing of modern English literary prose away from baroque complexity and rotund Johnsonian circuitousness toward smooth, straightforward journalistic directness. Nowhere is this more apparent than in the influence of his oft-reprinted essay, "Politics and the English Language" (1946), which quickly entered the curricula of secondary and university English syllabi. Here Orwell argued that all bad writing is morally wrong as well as politically and esthetically flawed. He also formulated six rules for good writing, which include: use short words instead of long ones, avoid foreign phrases, and cut words if you can do so. His sixth rule was typical of Orwell: break all of these rules rather than write something vulgar. In another Orwell touch, he disarmed the wary reader by noting that on "looking back through the essay" he had probably "committed the very faults I'm protesting against."[7]

Certain themes run through Orwell's oeuvre: his patriotism, his distrust of intellectuals, and his fear of a totalitarian future – especially, though not exclusively, its communist form. Orwell was that rare socialist who was internationalist and yet also patriotic. He was a cultural patriot, never a nationalist or jingoist, a champion of what biographer Bernard Crick called a "gentler patriotism."[8] Orwell's love for all things English, above all the countryside and native customs and habits, runs through his writing. In his first literary success, *Down and Out in Paris and London* (1933), Orwell revealed this deep affection (and also gave evidence of his growing talent for descriptive prose). After his year in Paris in 1928–29, there were many things that made him glad to be in England once more, he wrote, among them "bathrooms, armchairs, mint sauce, new potatoes properly cooked, brown bread, marmalade, beer made with veritable hops..." He added a typical Orwell caveat: "if you can pay for them."[9]

Orwell's patriotism served to divide him from his fellow socialists. His conversion was a gradual process that began in the early 1930s when he first encountered poverty among tramps and the destitute. At first there was a strong Tory anarchist element in his make-up, a William Cobbett-like anger toward the Establishment. As he noted in *The Road to Wigan Pier:* "For a long time, I seemed to spend half my time denouncing the insolence of bus drivers and the other half denouncing the evils of capitalism."

A pair of transformative events in Orwell's life led him to embrace socialism fully: his first-hand experience of mass unemployment and suffering in the coal-mining regions of the north of England and his soldiering in the Spanish Civil War. They turned Orwell into a committed, if idiosyncratic, man of the left. He would later write that it was in Spain that he became a convinced socialist. Yet in Britain his democratic socialism remained suspect on the Marxist left throughout his life and after.

When Orwell returned from the civil war in Spain in 1937, he sought to tell what he had witnessed, particularly the betrayal of the revolution by the Stalinists. Orwell had concluded that fighting fascism required opposing or exposing all forms of totalitarianism, including communism. As he later wrote in an essay on the writer Arthur Koestler, "The sin of nearly all left wingers from 1933 onwards is that they wanted to be anti-fascist without being anti-totalitarian."[10]

When Orwell tried to get that message out, the London literary left blocked him. His articles and reviews were rejected by the leading leftwing journal in England, *New Statesman.* Orwell never forgave those who sought to silence him. The whole experience only deepened his suspicion of those who exercised power, political and cultural. The roots of *Animal Farm* and *Nineteen Eighty-Four* can be found in Orwell's experiences in Spain and afterward in England.

Orwell's patriotism came to the fore most strongly in the early years of World War II. He had briefly flirted with pacifism, even joining the leftwing (yet anti-war) Independent Labour Party in 1938. But when the war broke out in September 1939, he knew that he would fight even if it meant defending "the bad [English capitalism] against the worst [fascism]."[11] In an essay about his rejection of pacifism, "My Country Right or Left," Orwell wrote that the war showed him that he "was a patriot at heart, would not sabotage or act against my own side, would support the war, would fight in it if possible."[12]

During the first two years of the war (1939–41), Orwell believed that there was a realistic chance for a revolutionary change to socialism in England. He hoped that the dangerous, near-fatal crisis that England faced in 1940 would lead the heretofore opposed working and middle classes to understand their fates as linked.

This never developed, and Orwell as a result soon turned to the issue that came to obsess him – his fear of communism and the related loss of the concept of objective truth. Almost all of his writings in the last years of his life revolve around these two themes. In 1944 he told a friend that "the willingness to criticize Russia and Stalin is the test of intellectual honesty."[13]

In the postwar years, *Animal Farm* and *Nineteen Eighty-Four* firmly established Orwell's reputation as a writer. The satirical portrait of the betrayal of the Russian Revolution in the form of an animal fable showed that Orwell's literary talents were on a par with one of his idols, Jonathan Swift. *Animal Farm* was Orwell's first literary triumph. It not only became a worldwide bestseller and made Orwell rich, but it also won him a wide audience for his views on the corruption of the language. Essays such as "Politics and the English Language," "Notes on Nationalism," "Second Thoughts on James Burnham," "Politics versus Literature" – all written around the same time as *Animal Farm* – demonstrate that Orwell, more than any contemporary writer, recognized how the very concept of historical truth was disappearing.

*Nineteen Eighty-Four* was written in the late 1940s, during which time Orwell battled the tuberculosis that would eventually kill him. His nightmarish portrait of the near-future is terrifying. Through the experience of its protagonist, Winston Smith, *Nineteen Eighty-Four* sketched out what the totalitarian specter threatened. Truth would disappear, history would be rewritten, individual identity would be smothered by the state, and sheer terror would rule. "If you want to imagine the future," Orwell wrote, "imagine a boot stomping on a human face."[14] It was as if Orwell was saying there would be no future, that indeed history itself would cease. Appearing as it did as the Cold War commenced, *Nineteen Eighty-Four* struck many readers as a prophecy, which only added to the book's impact.

Orwell was actually not as pessimistic as the doomsayers and alarmists. The novel itself holds out a margin of hope – the "proles" would represent the hope for the future. After Orwell's death, some commentators argued that he himself had lost all hope, an interpretation undermined by the fact that he was actively sketching new projects – a long essay on Evelyn Waugh among them. As he remarked on his deathbed to a friend, he believed he would not die so long as he had another book in him. That proved to be a false prophecy. He died of a severe hemorrhage of the lung on January 21, 1950.

Yet his literary fame was just beginning, and he has experienced an afterlife not only unique among English authors of his generation, but indeed unprecedented among modern writers in any language. His work has become so deeply imprinted in the cultural imagination that Orwell today occupies a status in the contemporary *Zeitgeist* comparable to Milton, Dickens, and even Shakespeare in earlier centuries – and, unlike them, a place not confined to the medium of literature or to the English-speaking world.

## Chapter 1

# Life and context

## Background and schooldays

George Orwell was born Eric Arthur Blair on June 25, 1903, in Motihari in the eastern part of Bengal Province, India. (For consistency, we will refer to Eric Blair as George Orwell throughout despite the fact that he didn't adopt that pen name until 1933.) Orwell would carefully categorize his family as "lower upper middle class," typical of his fascination with all matters relating to class. His family background was rather better than that. One ancestor on his father's side had married a daughter of the Earl of Westmoreland. Orwell's father, Richard Walmsley Blair, was descended from an eighteenth-century family that had made its living in the expansion of the British Empire. Richard Blair was born in 1857 and joined the Indian Civil Service in 1875 as an agent in the Opium Department. He served in that capacity with moderate success until his retirement in 1912.

Although she also was born in England, Ida Limouzin, Orwell's mother, was of French descent. The Limouzin family had settled in the Far East where they were engaged in the timber business in Burma. While on a trip to India, Ida Limouzin met and married Richard Blair who was eighteen years her senior. The marriage was a typical late Victorian arrangement. Two children were born in India: Marjorie in 1898 and Eric five years later. In 1904 Orwell's mother took the two children to England where they settled in Henley-on-Thames in Oxfordshire. Orwell would not see his father again until he was eight years old except for a brief visit in 1907 when his sister, Avril, was conceived. The lack of a male authority figure would have consequences later in Orwell's life.

In adulthood Orwell often spoke as if his family's financial position was precarious. This is hardly correct. His father's pension of over £400 was more than enough to provide a comfortable level of life.[1] The family moved about frequently, renting large homes in respectable neighborhoods.

Eric was the middle child, with one sister five years older and another five years younger. He was never very family oriented though he was closer to his mother than his father. With his father in India, Eric was raised in a feminine atmosphere by his mother, her sisters, and his two female siblings. This situation created certain tensions. On the one hand he liked women and enjoyed being spoiled by them. On the other he took them for granted, but he never really understood the feminine mind. His novels reveal an inability to penetrate the female mind. Dorothy in *A Clergyman's Daughter*, Rosemary in *Keep the Aspidistra Flying*, and even Julia in *Nineteen Eighty-Four* are caricatures created by a male mind that doesn't understand women.[2]

Eric's first years were happy. He loved the Oxfordshire countryside, enjoying hunting, fishing, swimming, and just rambling about. His youth established his love of nature. He kept rabbits, dogs, and all kinds of pets. He collected butterflies and developed affection for the plants and flowers of his native England. He never lost this love of the simple things of nature. His journalism shows both sensitivity to the environment far ahead of its time and a love for the plain names of English flowers.

As a young boy he formed a close friendship with a family nearby, the Buddicoms, whose daughter, Jacintha, became his first love. He led the Buddicom children on expeditions around the countryside and was the neighborhood leader in games. Jacintha discovered years later that the famous author of *Animal Farm* was the Eric Blair she knew. She got in touch with him and they exchanged letters. Her affectionate portrait of the young Eric in *Eric and Us* published in 1974 remains one of our best sources for his youth, counteracting many of his claims of a gloomy childhood.[3]

Ida Blair often read aloud to Eric during his early boyhood. He was fascinated by stories and by the sounds of certain words and wrote a poem when he was a child which compared the spokes of a chair to tigers' teeth, an allusion that showed some facility with words and was probably borrowed from William Blake's poem "The Tiger."

Young Orwell was a voracious reader. Kipling, Jack London, Shaw, and especially H. G. Wells fascinated him. From them he absorbed a portrait of a rich, smug Edwardian world that was in need of radical change. Like many bright children he never lost the sense of wonder at the world that reading opened for him. He would remain an Edwardian radical for the rest of his life. In the words of his friend Cyril Connolly: Orwell was "a revolutionary in love with 1910."[4]

At four Orwell was sent to a small school in the neighborhood run (according to Gordon Bowker's biography of Orwell) by French Ursuline nuns in Henley. Bowker's discovery of Orwell's exposure to Catholic nuns is interesting in light of his later rabid anti-Catholicism. Orwell made no mention of this experience in any of his writings.[5] Because he was precocious, arrangements were made when he was eight to send him to St. Cyprian's, a good preparatory school, near Eastbourne in Sussex.

St. Cyprian's was run by a husband and wife team, the Wilkes. The school had a reputation for producing scholars and winning places at some of the best English public schools including Eton and Harrow. Orwell's fees were reduced in the hope that he might he win a scholarship.

Orwell's experience at St. Cyprians constitutes one of the most controversial periods in his life. In his essay "Such, Such Were the Joys," written (according to Sir Bernard Crick) in 1940 not 1947 as the *Collected Essays, Journalism and Letters* states, Orwell portrays the harm preparatory schools (or "filthy private schools") could do to young boys on the brink of maturity.

Orwell was desperately unhappy at St. Cyprian's. He felt that he was an outsider among the sons of the rich. The portrait of the school and in particular of the Wilkes, whom he nicknamed "Sambo" and "Flip" in his essay, is unforgettable in its negativity. Vivid images such as the swimming bath with a turd floating in it, ceramic bowls with clotted stale bits of oatmeal on the rim, canings by Sambo and psychological intimidation by Flip have made "Such, Such Were the Joys" one of Orwell's most studied writings. Some commentators argue that the dark aspects of the essay foreshadow the world of *Nineteen Eighty-Four*.

Others go even further and note the date given in the *Collected Essays* for the essay, 1947, and then connect "Such, Such Were the Joys" to the writing of Orwell's dystopian novel. To disprove this Crick went to great lengths in an Appendix to his biography of Orwell to show that the essay was written earlier, possibly in 1940.[6] There are questions about the essay's accuracy. Others who attended St. Cyprian's had fonder memories of the school and the Wilkes, but throughout his life Orwell never deviated from his opinion that preparatory schools harmed young boys.

Whatever psychological damage St. Cyprian's inflicted on Orwell it enabled him to win a scholarship to both Wellington College and Eton. He left St. Cyprian's possessing a store of memories that he would draw upon as a writer later in life.

Orwell attended Wellington for nine weeks but was unhappy with the military atmosphere and the false patriotism he found there. He transferred to Eton as soon as an opening developed. He was a King's Scholar in the class of 1916, one of seventy young men set apart from the thousand or so that made up Eton's student body. Unlike at St. Cyprian's where he worked hard, he slacked off badly at Eton. He learned little, largely educating himself, reading widely and doing only that school work which interested him. He became fluent in French but did poorly in most other subjects and was satisfied to finish in the lower part of his class throughout his five years at Eton.

Although an outsider, Orwell was happy at Eton. The school left the students alone to progress as they saw fit. Orwell made a handful of friends there such as Cyril Connolly, who would later figure prominently in his literary career, and Steven Runciman, the future historian of the Crusades. Orwell had developed a sense of privacy that enabled him to keep a separate set of friends, a quality that he would follow for the rest of his life.

At Eton, Orwell cultivated the role of the cynic and rebel which suited his persona, fueled by his sense of being a poor boy among the sons of the rich. He was painfully sensitive about his family's social and financial status and was embarrassed when they visited him on parents' day. This sense of alienation was not as great as at St. Cyprian's, a testament to Eton's ability to make room for the rebels. While at Eton he took up smoking for the first time, which contributed to the bouts of bronchitis that would plague him for the rest of his life.

Orwell had told Jacintha Buddicom that someday he would become a famous writer. He filled notebooks with poetry, short stories, and essays, and occasionally contributed to various Eton publications. Orwell was filing away memories and developing that sense of the ironic observer that would characterize much of his later literary work.

World War I overshadowed his days at Eton. He joined the Officers Training Corps which prepared the junior officers for the coming campaigns. But by the time he was old enough to understand the full ramifications of the war, he and his generation were alienated by the crude patriotism and absurd propaganda of the government. Later he would say that every educated young man of his generation was a socialist. In reality, he was part of the vanguard of the alienated and the disenchanted, imitation Lytton Stracheys who flourished in the postwar milieu.

When it came to planning his future, Orwell was not sure what direction he wanted to take. Many of his Eton contemporaries went up to Oxford or Cambridge, but given his mediocre academic record that was out of the question for him. Sometime in 1921 he decided to take the examinations for the Indian Civil Service, thus following in his father's footsteps. Some commentators believe Orwell's decision was an attempt to win his father's respect. But unlike his father he chose to join the Indian Imperial Police not the Opium Department. He may have been the only Etonian to ever make this career move. Michael Shelden, in his authorized biography of Orwell, believes that his decision was a compound of the prestige and respect that being a policeman would engender.[7] The job also was lucrative. His salary would be £400 a year, a figure that almost matched his father's pension.

Bowker's biography attributes this choice to Orwell's belief that he had missed out on a great moment in history in being too young for World War I. Orwell believed that his generation really had not been tested.[8] Serving in the British Empire would compensate for this loss. At the very least, the Empire would provide a new adventure for the young Orwell. He was of two minds about the British Empire. As a budding radical he saw it as a sham, while his family's past, his reading of Kipling, Rider Haggard, and others gave the Empire a romantic gloss.

In August 1921 Orwell passed the entrance exam for the Indian Civil Service easily, doing particularly well in English and French and surprisingly well in the Latin and Greek that he had neglected since St. Cyprian's. As to his posting, he chose Burma, not the more desirable India, giving as his reason that he had family roots there. Two months later, in October 1921, the eighteen-year-old Orwell sailed for Burma to take up his post as an imperial policeman, a position that was to be one of the defining moments of his young life.

## Burma and "the wasted years"

Orwell described his time in Burma as "five wasted years." These five years witnessed the crystallization of his decision to become a writer. His time in Burma also provided him with a storehouse of memories that he would draw upon for the rest of his life. Like Kipling who spent just twelve of his seventy-one years in the East but drew upon them again and again, Orwell did the same. From these "wasted years" he would produce a novel, *Burmese Days*, and two classic essays, "A Hanging" and "Shooting an Elephant," that defined his unique documentary prose style.

Burma in October 1921 was in ferment. It had been annexed to the British Empire only in 1886 and was not integrated into England's imperial center-piece, India. When after the war the British attempted to placate Indian nationalism by granting a degree of governmental participation, Burma was not included. The first stirrings of a nationalist revolt began in Burma during the years that Orwell served there.

In his five years in Burma Orwell moved around from station to station. He was one of just ninety English imperial policemen. Along with a 13,000-man native constabulary, the English officers policed a nation of 13 million Burmese. Despite his later protests about his time in Burma, Orwell apparently was a competent policeman who was promoted for his work. Although a young man, he eventually came to administer large areas of Burmese territory. Orwell would later denigrate his time in Burma, but as Shelden points out it was a remarkable time for such a young man. Between the ages of nineteen and twenty-four, "while some of his old friends from Eton were still struggling to complete their university degrees, he was overseeing life-and-death matters for a population that was equal to that of a medium size European city." Whatever else it did, Burma matured Orwell.[9]

Orwell made no lasting friendships while serving in Burma. Instead, he honed his keen powers of observation and analysis as he studied the Burmese people (even mastering some Burmese dialects) and their English masters. Early in his tenure he realized he had made a mistake by joining the police. He was unhappy and although he had family in Burma he seems hardly to have bothered with them. He always remained something of an odd man out.

Orwell slowly began to reassess his life and at some point determined to chuck up his position. Pride kept him in Burma at first but there came a time when he knew he had to leave. He began to hate police work, believing that ruling over a native people was a racket, as corrupting for the ruler as the ruled. Burma was destroying him. "I felt that I had to got to escape," he later wrote, "not merely from imperialism but from every form of man's dominion over man."[10] This would be the motif of the next decade of his life. The hatred of authority that periodically flashed out during his school years now was focused on all the British Empire stood for. He wanted to write and believed he would never be able to do so in Burma. In 1927 he decided to resign and return to England.

> To put it mildly Burma and the Police did not live up to his [Orwell's] expectations. Within a year, despite a congenial posting he appears to have become entirely disenchanted with Burma and with his role as a policeman. He felt himself isolated from fellow expatriates . . . from the local Burmese . . . and above all from the values of imperialism. Etonian friend Christopher Hollis met Orwell in Burma whilst on his way to Australia and noted later that Orwell seemed to be a man divided between the conventional policeman and the radical critic of imperialism.[11]

Orwell returned to England in late 1927. His family was shocked to learn that he had no intention of resuming his career in Burma. Relations between

Orwell and his parents were strained once he told them that he intended to become a writer. The idea sounded bizarre. According to Avril, Orwell's mother was "horrified" at the idea of throwing away his career.[12]

For the next five years Orwell struggled to learn his craft. At first he wanted to be a novelist. He wrote short stories and plays, and even attempted a novel because that's what writers did. But he was dissatisfied with his efforts. These years provided Orwell with new experiences and adventures that he would draw upon as he did with his time in Burma. The next five years would also see the emergence of Orwell's unmatched literary talent as well as his discovery of his unique voice.

In 1927 and 1928 Orwell began the first of his expeditions into the world of the lowest in English society, the desperately poor, the unemployed, and even the tramps. Inspired by his literary hero Jack London's book *The People of the Abyss* (1903), Orwell mingled with the poor in London's East End to discover what their world was like. Orwell said he wanted to purge himself of the guilt that he had from his time in Burma and immerse himself among those English regarded as failures. He also was struggling to learn his craft, writing up his adventures but without any sense of direction or success at publication.

In the spring of 1928, following in the footsteps of the so-called "Lost Generation," he decided to move to Paris. France in the late 1920s was cheap and his savings from his time in Burma would last longer there. He lived in the Latin Quarter and wandered about the city while he continued to write. He mentions that he thought he saw James Joyce in the café of Les Deux Magots and lived just a few streets from where Ernest Hemingway resided at that time.

His Aunt Nellie Limouzin and her companion, Eugene Adam, active in the Esperanto movement, lived there and introduced him to some of their bohemian friends. These contacts led to Orwell's first published writings. In October 1928 he wrote an article on censorship in England for Henri Barbusse's radical leftwing weekly, *Monde*. Two months later, his first publication in England appeared in *G.K.'s Weekly* about a populist rightwing French journal, *L'Ami du Peuple*. This essay of a little over a thousand words shows Orwell struggling to gain his unique perspective. It is clearly written in Orwell's direct style and already shows him seeking a deeper meaning in a simple example of popular culture, in this case a semi-fascist journal that sought to provoke the poor.

In March of 1929 Orwell became seriously ill. He was admitted to the hospital, diagnosed with a serious case of influenza and placed in a ward for the poor. It was typical of Orwell that he would file away his hospitalization, especially the conditions in his ward, for a later essay, "How the Poor Die." The essay shows the skill that Orwell had already developed for revealing the grimmer side of life. For Orwell there was always a general lesson to be learned in any specific experience. He may have missed out on a university education but he was getting a more interesting education in life.

Orwell would struggle for the next year to find outlets for his writing. He was gaining confidence and, more significantly, reshaping some of his earlier writings into a serious book, the forerunner of his first major publication, *Down and Out in Paris and London*.

He remained in Paris for the rest of 1929 revising his long manuscript. He contributed an occasional piece to *Monde* but spent most of his time working on *Down and Out*.

For a time Orwell worked as a dishwasher or *plongeur* at a Parisian hotel. He wrote in *Down and Out* that his money had been stolen by a prostitute and he was forced to take this desperate job. He was never destitute as he could always have turned to his Aunt or Eugene Adam for funds to tide him over.

The *plongeur* story raises questions about the historicity of *Down and Out*. Most commentators believe it a blend of fact and fiction. But a copy of *Down and Out* that Orwell had given to one of his women friends, Brenda Salkeld, later surfaced. There are notes in his handwriting confirming many of the incidents in the book.[13]

After eighteen months in Paris, Orwell decided to return to England in December 1929. His reasons are not clear, but he was homesick and wanted to be back in England. He also was inspired by a bit of good fortune. An essay on living with tramps, "The Spike," which he had sent to Max Plowman, the editor of the literary journal *Adelphi*, had been accepted. Orwell packed up his notebooks, his book-length manuscript, and his memories of Paris and returned home. In *Down and Out* he recorded how pleased he was to be getting back to English soil: "England is a very good country when you are not poor."[14]

Orwell's formative education was over. He had completed his Oxford and Cambridge and was about to take the next steps in the creation of a major literary figure.

## The struggle to become a writer

Orwell returned to England in 1930 determined to pursue a writing career. He believed that serious writers wrote fiction. Later he would claim that he wanted to write "enormous naturalistic novels with unhappy endings." Orwell's models were the successful novelists he read in huge numbers throughout his early years: Kipling, John Galsworthy, H. G. Wells, D. H. Lawrence, and particularly Somerset Maugham. He particularly admired Maugham's ability to tell "a story straight-forwardly and without frills." As Michael Levenson has noted, Orwell "was drawn to the glamour of authorship and for him the glamour belonged not to journalism but to novel writing."[15] It would take him half a decade to learn where his real talents lay.

During the next six years of his life Orwell would struggle to find his voice. He failed to recognize that his skills were best directed to documentary prose and journalism that he regarded as hack work. Orwell wrote constantly and prodigiously. It is doubtful that there was any time when he wasn't writing, trying to learn his craft.

> All of his [Orwell's] books are obviously based upon his own experiences, and it is clear that he deliberately went out to gain experiences in order to write about them. This is customary and raises no problem in writers of travel books. But Orwell was primarily a traveler through his own land, through his own society and his own memories. As V. S. Pritchett said, he was "a writer who has gone native" in his own country.[16]

Between 1933 and 1937 Orwell would produce a book a year: three novels and two prose masterpieces. He also produced over fifty essays and book reviews for *Adelphi*, where he found a sympathetic home for his work. The editor, Max Plowman, encouraged him as did his successors, J. Middleton Murry and especially Sir Richard Rees. Rees was a fellow Etonian and the first person Orwell felt comfortable with culturally and intellectually. Toward the end of his life Orwell would make Rees his literary executor, a sign of his confidence in Rees's judgment.

On his return to England Orwell had to find work. His money had run out. He lived with his parents in Southwold for a time, but then began a series of dead-end jobs: taking care of a mentally disabled child, serving as a monitor for two young boys, teaching at two seedy boys' schools, and finally working in a bookshop in London. All the while he continued his writing.

Orwell returned to England with a manuscript of his adventures in Paris and London that he was still revising. He also had a partial draft of a novel about Burma, loosely based on his own experiences. Although he was dismissive about much that he wrote – a characteristic that he would carry over for the rest of his life – he was gaining confidence in his literary powers. Except for *Animal Farm*, Orwell rarely expressed satisfaction about anything he wrote. Even "A Hanging" and "Shooting an Elephant," which were written during these years, were passed off by Orwell lightly. When John Lehmann, editor of *New Writing*, solicited a piece, Orwell sent him "Shooting an Elephant," along with a half-apology that it wasn't very good.[17] Orwell's dismissal of his work functioned as a protective device. Late in life he spoke very critically of much of his literary output, even describing two of his novels (*A Clergyman's Daughter* and *Keep the Aspidistra Flying*) as failures.

During 1930–31 Orwell reworked the manuscript of his Paris and London experiences. He lacked confidence in the project, especially when two publishers, Jonathan Cape and Faber and Faber, rejected it. What made the latter rejection especially painful was that it was done by a writer whom Orwell deeply admired, T. S. Eliot, who judged the manuscript too short and its two halves disconnected. Orwell abandoned the manuscript, telling one of his friends, Mabel Fierz, to destroy it while saving the paper clips. Instead, Fierz took the manuscript to a literary agent, Leonard Moore, who soon found a publisher, Victor Gollancz.[18] Gollancz owned a small leftwing publishing house with a reputation for recognizing unusual books. Moore wrote Orwell the good news in June 1932. Gollancz gave him an advance of £40, a modest sum which indicates that he was hedging his bets about the book's success.

In January 1933 the book – bearing the final title of *Down and Out in Paris and London* – was published. At first Orwell wanted it published anonymously as he wasn't proud of the effort. In reality he didn't want his parents to know that he was the author of such a bohemian – and depressing – book. Orwell suggested simply using X, but Gollancz insisted on a real name. After considering a number of alternatives, the author selected "George Orwell" – "George" because it was a common English name; "Orwell" for a little river in Suffolk near his Southwold home. Although he would use both names occasionally, and write book reviews under his birth name until the late 1930s, from a literary standpoint he was George Orwell. *Down and Out* sold 3,500 copies in Britain and another 1,400 in the American edition, which appeared six months year later. Gollancz, who was shrewd businessman, believed he had stumbled upon a potentially successful author.

At the time of the publication of *Down and Out,* Orwell informed Moore that he had completed more than 100 pages of his novel about his days in Burma. Three months later he had written another 100 pages. He finished the book in July 1933 and sent it on to Gollancz. Orwell felt that he had failed in what he set out to do, bemoaning in his typical fashion that "there are great wads of it I hate."[19]

Fearing the possibilities of libel, Gollancz rejected *Burmese Days*. Later he admitted that he made a mistake, calling *Burmese Days* "an exceptionally brilliant book." Moore secured a contract from Harper's, the American firm that had published *Down and Out. Burmese Days* was published in the United States in October 1934.

After Orwell made changes to deal with libel problems, Gollancz agreed to publish *Burmese Days* in England. It appeared in June 1935. Gollancz was now convinced that he had a new author in his stable who would become a "successful" (i.e., widely selling) author.

While waiting for the publication of *Burmese Days*, Orwell began yet another novel. Entitled *A Clergyman's Daughter*, it attempted to integrate some of his experiences of living on the fringes of society with the travails of a young woman trying to escape a life of frustration. The novel was an unsuccessful effort to enter into the mind of a woman. One scene set in Trafalgar Square among the tramps where the protagonist is suffering from amnesia shows the influence of James Joyce's "Ulysses in Nighttown" scene on Orwell.

*A Clergyman's Daughter* was published in March 1935 after Orwell had moved to London to work in a bookstore, Booklover's Corner in Hampstead. Sales were discouraging: fewer than 2,000 copies in England and a mere 400 in the United States.

Orwell spent sixteen months living in London, a city he disliked. And yet these months would prove crucial for his career and his life. He would write another novel loosely based on his experiences in the bookshop, meet his future wife and start off on the journey to the north of England that would bring him his first big sales success – and his first round of literary controversy.

## Literary breakthrough

The years 1935–37 witnessed the final maturation of George Orwell. Even before the mid-1930s, his literary output was impressive – two books, a handful of essays plus some reviews. But now for the first time he would come to be taken seriously as a writer.

Shortly after Orwell arrived in London he began work on yet another traditional novel, *Keep the Aspidistra Flying*. He had been unhappy with *A Clergyman's Daughter* believing that he made "a muck of it." He told his former girlfriend, Brenda Salkeld, that he wanted his new novel "to be a work of art."[20] Orwell was determined to produce a major work of fiction set in the midst of England's worst economic slump, a Depression era version of Wells's *History of Mr. Polly*.

While he was living in London, Orwell came into contact with other members of the literary establishment who would prove important in shaping his intellectual development. He reestablished contact with Cyril Connolly, who had been at school with him and who was developing a reputation as a rising star in the London literary firmament. Connolly would play a major role in advancing Orwell's career. Orwell deepened his friendship with Sir Richard Rees and met Geoffrey Gorer, the anthropologist and writer, who particularly prized *Burmese Days*. He also received a flattering letter from the novelist Anthony Powell praising his writing. They would become close friends during the war.

Orwell worked at the bookshop and spent much of his free time writing. He made great progress and was happy with what he called "my good old novel." *Keep the Aspidistra Flying* was published by Victor Gollancz in April 1936, thirteen months after Orwell had started it, which is remarkable considering that he was holding down a job and doing book reviews for the *New English Weekly*, a Quaker leftwing journal edited by Philip Mairet. Orwell had drifted away from *Adelphi* because it was having internal problems.

Orwell's new novel sold approximately 2,500 copies. No American publisher expressed interest in it, perhaps because it was so negative in tone and atmosphere.

There is an autobiographical element in everything that Orwell wrote, none more so than *Keep the Aspidistra Flying*. Some commentators regard the protagonist, Gordon Comstock, the failed poet forced to work in a bookshop and hating every moment of it, as a thinly veiled version of Orwell himself. Comstock's complaints about modern society and grumbling about not being able to make a decent living resemble Orwell's attitudes. Unlike Orwell's early novels, however, *Keep the Aspidistra Flying* has a happy ending. Gordon ends up marrying his pregnant girlfriend, Rosemary, accepting his new role as husband and father, and living a bourgeois life in a flat on the Edgware Road.

Orwell might have been inclined to end *Keep the Aspidistra Flying* on a positive note because he fell in love while writing the novel. In March 1935, Orwell met Eileen O'Shaughnessy, a student in psychology at University College London. It was love at first sight on Orwell's part – he told his friend the writer Rayner Heppenstall that Eileen was "the nicest person I have met in a long time."[21] In fact, he proposed marriage within a couple of weeks of meeting her. She wasn't sure and put off the decision. But they were married a year after they first met.

Eileen was a decisive influence on Orwell's literary and professional career as well as on his personal life. A sophisticated, well-educated woman, she found him eccentric and opinionated. Instead of trying to change him, she encouraged these qualities. She was amused by the odd things he would say and do. Friends who knew them both said that she loved him and that he came to depend on her. He respected her judgment on literary matters and on people. It was a happy, rather unconventional, marriage.

The appearance of three Orwell novels in 1935–36 marked his arrival as a serious literary figure. His books were reviewed with respect, if not admiration, in the best newspapers and magazines by some of the leading literary figures in England – Compton Mackenzie, Cyril Connolly, and William Plomer among others.

A sign of his arrival as a serious writer was an invitation in May 1936 by the well-known literary figure John Lehmann to contribute an essay to *Penguin New Writing*. Orwell didn't respond at first but then agreed. He told Lehmann that the piece he had in mind, based on an incident that had taken place in Burma, might not suit the new magazine. "I mean it might be too low brow for your paper & I doubt whether there is anything anti-Fascist in the shooting of an elephant."[22] Lehmann was wise enough to take a chance and for his pains got one of Orwell's greatest and most reprinted essays, "Shooting an Elephant."

By this time Orwell was restless. After finishing *Keep the Aspidistra Flying*, Gollancz approached him with an idea. He wanted Orwell to write a book about conditions among the worst victims of the Depression. What Gollancz had in mind was a documentary work of investigation not another novel. The proposal was inspired, and it showed that Gollancz's literary instincts were sharp. Orwell jumped at the chance. In early 1936, with a small advance from Gollancz, he left for what Bernard Crick would call Orwell's "critical journey." As a result of Orwell's trip to the north of England, he completed the development of the unique documentary prose style that made him famous and gained his first great literary success.

Orwell would spend two months traveling through those parts of the north hardest hit by the Depression. He investigated housing conditions, lived in slums, and even went down a coal mine. He interviewed the unemployed, went to political meetings, and tried to get a feel for what poverty was like.

At first, Orwell did not have a clear idea of how he wanted to write up his research. Instead, he gathered information in the form of notes and a diary. The subsequent book, *The Road to Wigan Pier*, would bring Orwell critical plaudits and a degree of public renown for the first time. It would also prompt Orwell's decision to move away from traditional fiction into the area where his talents really lay: reportage. He had already shown signs of a documentary skill in some of his early essays such as "How the Poor Die," "A Hanging" and "Shooting an Elephant." Until now Orwell was still enamored by the idea of writing traditional novels.

Orwell wrote up the results of his investigation in an unusual way. The first part of *The Road to Wigan Pier* is a straightforward portrait of the conditions he uncovered, a savage critique of the evils of capitalism. It contains vivid images of life among the poor: scenes such as the tripe shop where he lived with its bluebottle flies, the urine-filled chamber pot under the kitchen table, and unforgettably his description of a woman trying to clean a clogged drainpipe. The latter passage warrants quoting at length as an example of Orwell's dramatic prose.

> At the back of one of the houses a young woman was kneeling on the stones, poking a stick up the leaden waste-pipe . . . I had time to see everything about her – her sacking apron, her clumsy clogs, her arms reddened by the cold. She looked up as the train passed, and I was almost near enough to catch her eye. She had a round pale face, the usual exhausted face of the slum girl who is twenty-five and looks forty, thanks to miscarriages and drudgery; and it wore, for the second in which I saw it, the most desolate, hopeless expression I have ever seen . . .[23]

Citing such passages in *Wigan Pier*, the American political journalist and critic Dwight Macdonald, in an essay analyzing Orwell and Trotsky as sociological reporters, would describe Orwell's work as superior to anything the old Bolshevik ever wrote.[24]

The second part of *The Road to Wigan Pier* contained Orwell's first serious attempt to analyze the flaws of socialism and socialists. Orwell was groping toward a political stance that still was not firm and secure in his own mind. He zeroed in on the ideological limitations of socialism and was especially effective in attributing its failure to win a large audience because of the strangeness of its adherents. The worst argument for socialism, he wrote, was its followers, that "dreary tribe" of Quakers, fruit juice drinkers, pacifists, nudists who repelled normal people.

*The Road to Wigan Pier* demonstrated the considerable talent that Orwell possessed for vivid writing and showed his rare gift as a controversialist. He argued, for example, that socialism in England would have no future unless it could win over the middle classes, showing them that they shared an interest with the working classes. This was an argument that Orwell also stressed during World War II, most notably in *The Lion and the Unicorn*, and in his essay "My Country Right or Left." His views contradicted Marxist thinking and showed impressive powers of analysis on his part. He made an unusual observation in *The Road to Wigan Pier* that also disputed Marxist doctrine. Fascism, he argued, did not represent capitalism in its death throes, as the Marxists believed, but was instead a revolutionary mass movement that eventually would challenge both capitalism and socialism. This was an insight that he would return to during the early stages of World War II.

After returning from his journey through the north, Orwell quickly wrote up his research. He had a manuscript ready for Gollancz by December 1936. Knowing that the book was not what Gollancz had in mind when he commissioned the project, Orwell worried that it might be rejected. He told his literary agent, Leonard Moore, that the manuscript was "too fragmentary and, on the surface, not very leftwing."[25]

Much to Orwell's surprise, Gollancz accepted the manuscript and even decided to publish it as one of the offerings of the newly founded Left Book Club. Gollancz recognized a potential bestseller even if he found parts of it distasteful. Making the book a choice of the Left Book Club guaranteed large sales as the Club's membership was around 40,000 to 50,000. Orwell had little time to ponder his new-found success, as he had decided on his next venture – a trip to Spain, which by 1936 was in the midst of one of the bloodiest civil wars in modern European history.

## Spain and Orwell's political education

For Orwell and many others of his generation, the Spanish Civil War would become the litmus test of the struggle against fascism. The Spanish war would divide English society and intellectual quarters as no other foreign policy issue had since the French Revolution. Orwell told one of his fellow Etonians, Denys King-Farlow, that he was following events in Spain closely. At this time Orwell's political views were vaguely leftwing, as the second half of *The Road to Wigan Pier* makes clear. While his denunciations of capitalism, materialism, and imperialism placed him squarely on the political left, he remained divided about what to advocate and what to support. His fellow worker at Booklover's Corner, Jon Kimche, described Orwell at this point as a kind of intellectual Tory anarchist.[26] Spain would change all that.

Hocking the family silver (according to Gordon Bowker) to pay for the trip, Orwell left for Spain around Christmas 1936.[27] He naïvely wanted to join the International Brigade. But they were controlled by communists – and Orwell was *persona non grata* in their eyes after *The Road to Wigan Pier*. The leader of the English communists, Harry Pollitt, refused any help. Orwell then approached the Independent Labour Party (ILP), securing letters of introduction from two of its leaders, Fenner Brockway and Noel Brailsford. Their assistance enabled Orwell to join a radical Spanish political militia, the POUM (The Workers' Party of Marxist Unification), a kind of sister organization to the ILP. The POUM was a uniquely Spanish amalgam of anarchism and Trotskyism, a group that perfectly suited Orwell's own political inclinations. It was Marxist yet vigorously anti-Stalinist.

Orwell stayed in Spain for almost half a year, spending almost four months at the front. He had gone out to write articles and do research for a book. But he also was determined to take part in the fighting. These six months would witness the transformation of Orwell into a full-scale, if idiosyncratic, socialist and, more importantly, a dedicated enemy of Stalinism.

Orwell arrived in Barcelona, the capital of Catalonia, while the revolution was at its peak. He was deeply moved by the egalitarian spirit of the city and its people. The atmosphere was exactly what he thought a revolutionary situation should be – no tipping, no aristocratic titles. Instead, everyone was "Comrade," even the prostitutes. Orwell was enchanted.

After a brief period of training, Orwell was sent to the Catalan front. He experienced some fighting there, but most of his time was sheer boredom, exacerbated by material deprivation. Given his ability to enjoy privations, Orwell passed the time with few complaints, devoting his energies to reading and writing whenever he could. He was laying the groundwork for another book.

Eileen came out in February 1937 and worked for the POUM in Barcelona. In May Orwell took leave. He arrived in Barcelona just as fighting broke out between the POUM and its allies against the new communist-dominated government. The five days of brutal fighting saw 400 people killed and more than 1,000 wounded. It was the final stage of Orwell's political education. He was shocked to see the POUM's followers hunted down and denounced as both enemies of the revolution and as *de facto* allies of the fascists.

Orwell returned to the Catalan front and on May 20, near Huesca, he was shot through the throat by a sniper. The wound was nearly fatal, narrowly missing his carotid artery. While recovering – he lost his voice for a time– Orwell discovered how dangerous any connection to the POUM had now become. POUM supporters were being rounded up and, in some cases, murdered by the communists. The opening of the Soviet archives after the collapse of communism has revealed that Orwell was targeted for execution. In June he and Eileen escaped from Spain and crossed into France by passing themselves off as English tourists.

When Orwell returned to England, he discovered that reports on the war in Spain had been distorted for ideological purposes. Spain had depressed him about the future victory of fascism, but it also had exhilarated him about the possibility of people acting together for revolutionary ends. He offered an essay to the *New Statesman*, "Spilling the Spanish Beans," on his experiences in Spain, but it was rejected by the editor, Kingsley Martin, on political grounds – it contradicted the party line that POUM, the anarchists, and Trotskyists were allies of fascism.

Orwell was outraged at British leftists both for parroting the Moscow line and for their attempts to suppress the truth of what was happening in Spain. He never forgave Martin, whose offer to pay him a kill fee for the rejected article Orwell called "hush money." Years later, when Orwell was having lunch with Malcolm Muggeridge, he asked him to change seats. When Muggeridge enquired why, Orwell said Martin was sitting across from him and he couldn't abide "looking at his corrupt face."[28]

Orwell began writing a book about his experiences in Spain. He also tried through his essays and reviews to publicize the true story of events there. Within a short time, Orwell had solidified his reputation as an independent, iconoclastic man of the left with his attacks on what he called the craven behavior of English leftwing intellectuals. After Spain, he told Cyril Connolly, he "really believed in Socialism."[29] But his Spanish activities also made him enemies who would pursue him for the rest of his career.

Orwell's Spanish testament, *Homage to Catalonia*, was written at a furious pace between July and December 1937. Orwell called it his best book up to that time. It related his personal experiences in Spain, set against the backdrop of a larger story, the betrayal of the revolution. It contained some trademark Orwell vignettes. For example, while serving as a sniper he saw a fascist soldier defecating, and couldn't bring himself to shoot him. Because a man with his trousers down wasn't a fascist, he wrote, but a fellow human being.

Orwell was determined to salvage the reputation of those anarchists and Trotskyists with whom he served. He was one of the first persons to note that the communists were not interested in a victory in Spain, but rather wanted to prolong the fighting in order both to weaken the fascists and to divert attention from what was happening in Stalin's Russia.

Under the terms of his contract with Gollancz, Orwell was obliged to offer him the book even though he suspected that it would be rejected because it was politically unacceptable. When Gollancz turned the manuscript down, Frederic Warburg, of small a publishing house, Secker & Warburg, agreed to print it.

*Homage to Catalonia* appeared in April 1938. Warburg printed 1,500 copies, of which only 800 were sold. The timing was bad. The English literary establishment didn't want to hear Orwell's message, calling him confused or politically naïve. As we will later discuss, the British left argued that POUM was in effect part of Franco's Fifth Column. Orwell was outraged and would never forgive those who denigrated those with whom he fought in Spain.

Orwell's friends wrote complimentary reviews but in insignificant journals that could not offset the impact of the negative notices. Orwell was angry. The episode confirmed his suspicions about most leftwing intellectuals. One positive note came in a letter from the novelist Herbert Read, who told Orwell that *Homage to Catalonia* was "as good as anything that came out of the Great War."[30]

[I]t was "other events" in 1936, not just the actual experience of "Wigan" but the reckoning it forced on him of where he stood, which committed him to Leftwing socialism and took him to Spain in the first place. He was committed to "democratic Socialism" ... before he went, but not to being against totalitarianism. It was Spain, not Wigan, that convinced him that the Communist Party was working irredeemably against the revolution and led him to see the similarities between Socialism and Hitlerism.[31]

Undermined by years of neglect and made worse by the harsh conditions in Spain, Orwell's health had broken down by the time *Homage to Catalonia* appeared. From March to September 1938 he lay in a sanatorium with tubercular lesions in his lungs. He was told by his doctors that in order to recover he should spend the winter in a warm climate. As he had no money, that was out of the question. But through the intercession of a literary acquaintance, Dorothy Plowman, the novelist L. H. Myers, an admirer of Orwell's work, anonymously advanced him £300. With his characteristic sense of rectitude, Orwell accepted the money as a loan and not a gift, promising to pay it back in the future.

Orwell and Eileen left for Morocco, eventually settling in Marrakech in September 1938 just as the Munich crisis reached its culmination. During his seven months in Morocco, Orwell worked on a new novel about an innocent lower-middle-class businessman trying to recapture his lost youth against the backdrop of the coming war.

*Coming Up for Air*, would become the last and, in many ways, the finest of Orwell's traditional novels. The protagonist, George Bowling, "a fat man with a thin man inside," was more likeable and human than the male protagonists of Orwell's other novels. Despite its implication that a terrible war is in the offing, *Coming Up for Air* has an optimistic quality about it. Bowling, the complacent lower-middle-class salesman, recognizes that, despite the changes that have overtaken his lost Edwardian ideal world, life must go on. He also understands that at some level, the future will require the middle and working classes to cooperate. If not, everything that England stands for will be lost. Through Bowling, Orwell is reiterating the message at the end of *The Road to Wigan Pier*: the middle classes have "nothing to lose but their aitches." *Coming Up for*

*Air* prefigures the argument that Orwell would make in the early, dark days of World War II, namely that only a revolution uniting the middle and working classes can save England.

Orwell and Eileen spent six and half months in Morocco, returning to England in March 1939, two weeks after Hitler had annexed the rump of the Czech state. The British public now felt betrayed and the drift to war became overwhelming. Orwell had completed *Coming Up for Air* while in Morocco. Even though he would have, after the controversy over *Homage to Catalonia*, preferred another publisher, he delivered a copy of the manuscript to Gollancz.

*Coming Up for Air* was published in June 1939, mostly to positive reviews. A critic for the *Observer* ended his review by calling Orwell "a great writer." The novel sold more than 3,000 copies, a decent figure. Both the review and the sales confirmed the growing opinion in literary circles in London that Orwell was a man to watch.

## Orwell's war

The years immediately before World War II were traumatic for Orwell. His health broke down again, requiring a long convalescence in a sanatorium. Spain had turned him into a committed socialist but he was disillusioned with the Popular Front mentality of "no enemies on the left" that prevailed in English intellectual circles. As a way of expressing his anger he formally joined the Independent Labour Party (ILP) on his return from Spain. The ILP was the most radical and pacifist of the leftwing parties. It argued that the drift to war had to be opposed because there was no difference between the capitalist democracies and the fascists. Any war between them, the ILP argued, would only see the triumph of fascism in some guise.

Orwell said that he had been convinced since 1936 that a war was coming. When it came he quickly shed his pacifism. He relates that when the Nazis and Soviets signed an alliance in August 1939 he knew he would fight. As he wrote in 1940 for John Lehmann's *Folios of New Writing*, the news of the Nazi–Soviet Pact proved that "the long drilling in patriotism which the middle classes go through had done its work, and that once England was in a serious jam it was impossible for me to sabotage it."[32] He would defend an England whose class system and materialism he despised. Like Guy Crouchback, the hero of Evelyn Waugh's *Sword of Honour* trilogy, Orwell would fight for one evil because it opposed a greater one.

During the years from 1939 to 1941 Orwell was searching for a way to contribute usefully to the war effort. His personal and family life was in upheaval. Eileen moved to London to take a job with the Censorship Department in Whitehall when the war broke out. She only came down to their house in Wallington every few weeks, which left Orwell lonely. He followed her to London late in 1939, committed to finding a way to contribute to the war effort.

Nevertheless he continued to write. Before the war broke out he had started writing a new short book, *Inside the Whale.* It consisted of three essays: a study of the popular comic magazines read by young boys, an interpretation of Charles Dickens, and a long analysis of the trends in literature in the 1920s and 1930s. One of the topics in the latter was the work of the American Henry Miller, whose writings were considered scandalous if not downright porno-graphic. Orwell admired Miller's honesty but argued that he couldn't follow Miller's advice of not paying attention to political developments. "We are moving into an age of totalitarian dictatorships – an age in which freedom of thought will be . . . a meaningless abstraction. The autonomous individual is going to be stamped out of existence."[33]

The Dickens essay and the study of boys' magazines were destined to become canonical. Orwell's Dickens essay has been cited in many academic studies of the great Victorian novelist. The piece "Boys' Weeklies" proved a landmark in what would become a new academic genre of popular culture studies. It was a serious cultural analysis of seemingly ephemeral material.

*Inside the Whale,* for which Orwell received an advance of just £20, was published by Gollancz in March 1940 just as the so-called the Phony War was about to end. Only 1,000 copies were printed and few sold. The collection only began to receive the attention it deserved after Orwell's death when an American edition was published.

When Orwell moved to London, he arranged to have the "Boys' Weeklies" essay published in Cyril Connolly's new venture, *Horizon.* It was the first of a series of major essays which Orwell published in a magazine that Evelyn Waugh described as "the outstanding publication of the decade." "Boys' Weeklies" was an analysis of English comic magazines such as the *Gem* and *Magnet,* a popular literature that fascinated Orwell with its unchanging Edwardian worldview. He enjoyed doing pieces like "Boys' Weeklies," which he labeled "semi-sociological literary criticism." But he told Leonard Moore that there was "very little money" in such work. Despite that fact, he would produce many more essays of that kind in the next few years.

By the spring of 1940, the war suddenly had taken a deadly turn for England. The German attack in the West beginning May 10 overran Holland, Belgium, and France in six weeks. By June, England was alone facing the seemingly invincible might of Nazi Germany. Orwell desperately wanted to be part of the struggle. He tried enlisting in the military in any capacity, but he was rejected due to his history of health problems. Eventually he joined the newly formed Home Guard and served for three years as a sergeant.

In a perverse way Orwell thoroughly enjoyed the war and its austerities. He found the events of 1940 reminiscent of his early days in Catalonia. His diary reveals Orwell's deeply patriotic side. When the British army was seemingly trapped on the beaches at Dunkirk, he noted – "Horrible as it is, I hope the BEF [British Expeditionary Forces] is cut to pieces sooner than capitulate."[34]

Although Orwell couldn't find an outlet for his desire to take part in the fighting, he stayed busy. In May, as a way of earning money, he accepted an offer from *Time and Tide*, a popular magazine he detested, to write film and play reviews. Eventually he would write more than two dozen reviews. He taught himself to write these reviews in one sitting so as not to waste valuable time. He was nothing if not prolific. In all he wrote over 100 articles, essays, and reviews for seven different periodicals in 1940.

In December 1940 he was approached by the American anti-Stalinist journal *Partisan Review* to write an occasional letter on what was happening "under the surface" in England during the war. The pay was cheap, just about $10 per letter. Orwell's *Partisan Review* letters – he wrote thirteen, the first in 1941, the last in 1946 – began making him known in American political and cultural circles.

Orwell was convinced that the war held the seeds of a great political reconstruction for England. He believed in a genuine revolution, one in which the working classes and middle classes would be united by their inherent patriotism. He now began writing an extended essay on this theme for a new series founded by Frederic Warburg, entitled Searchlight Books. Written in the midst of the Battle of Britain and the Blitz that followed in the fall of 1940, Orwell's contribution, *The Lion and the Unicorn*: *Socialism and English Genius*, appeared in February 1941.

*The Lion and the Unicorn* reflects the peak moment of Orwell's revolutionary patriotism. He believed that the crisis of 1940, during which England was threatened by invasion, created a genuine opportunity to bring about a revolution. Unlike France, which Orwell considered corrupt, England still possessed a moral center. For all their differences, the middle and working classes were willing to fight and die for England. He argued that the socialists should exploit this patriotism. A decent form of socialism was impossible, he believed, "without defeating Hitler, on the other hand we cannot defeat Hitler while we remain economically and socially in the nineteenth century."[35] He was calling for something like the old Trotskyist mantra: the war and revolution were inseparable. Winning one would lead to the triumph of the other.

*The Lion and the Unicorn* sold 12,000 copies, more than anything Orwell had written except for *The Road to Wigan Pier*. It also gained him further recognition. The reviews were overwhelmingly favorable. V. S. Pritchett compared him to George Bernard Shaw for his ability to upset traditional modes of thought. Other reviewers found the book a "must read," describing him as a brilliant writer with a "blunt and tenacious honesty of mind." Orwell was establishing himself as one of the best journalists of his time.

By the time that *The Lion and the Unicorn* appeared, Orwell no longer believed that a revolution was possible. He thought the revolutionary moment had passed during the crisis of the summer of 1940. Following the German attack on the Soviet Union in June 1941, Orwell watched as the leftwing intellectuals deserted the cause of revolution. Now all attention was on opening up a second front in order to save the Soviet Union. In his diary Orwell sardonically noted: "One could not have a better example of the moral and emotional shallowness of our time than the fact that we are now more or less pro-Stalin. This disgusting murderer is temporarily on our side, and so the purges etc. are forgotten." The left hero-worshiped Stalin, he argued, because they had "lost their patriotism and sense of religious belief while continuing to need a god and a fatherland."[36] Like Waugh's Guy Crouchback, the war had lost some of its flavor for Orwell.

On June 25, 1941–four days after the German attack on the Soviet Union– Orwell was offered a job as a BBC talks assistant for India and the Far East. The pay was good, £640 per year, which brought him an income comparable to what he had earned when he left the Imperial Police in Burma. Along with his wife's salary the Orwell's could afford to live a middle-class life in London. Although they often had to change residences because they were bombed out, they maintained a comfortable existence in flats throughout London, which enabled them to have dinner parties for Orwell's expanding circle of friends.

Orwell spent twenty-seven months at the BBC, largely wasted months in his view, broadcasting a variety of programs to an almost non-existent Indian audience. He did the job well and was a good administrator and an easy boss. He enjoyed the opportunity of enlisting famous writers such as T. S. Eliot, Dylan Thomas, J. B. Priestley, and others to do his broadcasts, and he showed imagination in his programming. But radio broadcasting wasn't his métier. He found his life at the BBC increasingly bothersome, describing the place as "a mixture of whoreshop and lunatic asylum." He soon wanted out, complaining that he was unable to write a book while laboring for the BBC.

What is nonetheless remarkable is how much he did write during those twenty-seven months. He found time to produce six long "London Letters" for the *Partisan Review* as well as a number of book reviews for the *Observer* and other journals. He also published some of his classic essays during his time at the BBC. For instance, "Wells, Hitler and World State," and "The Art of Donald McGill," appeared in *Horizon* in August and September 1941. Connolly provided an outlet for some of Orwell's best work during this time, including an appreciation of T. S. Eliot's edition of Kipling's poetry.

Two other major essays were written during Orwell's time at the BBC. "The Rediscovery of Europe," a talk given by Orwell on the BBC, was published by *The Listener*. "Looking Back on the Spanish War," his reflection on the political and cultural distortions of the Spanish Civil War, appeared in a small socialist journal in 1943.

## Last years

By the summer of 1943 Orwell had had enough of radio propaganda and was frustrated because he hadn't written a new book. He believed he had not done enough for the war effort and was pondering the idea of becoming a war correspondent, an assignment he finally received during the last months of the war in Europe. It proved one of the few literary tasks at which he was not successful.

Orwell had plans for a new book that had been percolating his mind during his months at the BBC. He had begun *Animal Farm* at this time and wanted more time to work on it and on his other literary ideas. In his letter of resignation to the BBC in September 1943, Orwell registered no complaints, simply saying he believed he was wasting both his time and the government's money doing work for which he wasn't suitable.

Two months later he was asked to replace John Atkins as literary editor of the leftwing paper, *Tribune*, a task far more suitable to his talents and interests than the BBC. He was comfortable with *Tribune's* political stance, a kind of aggressive leftism, plus he enjoyed the literary freedom that he was granted. He could write what he wanted and he published a startling number of reviews, articles, and essays during his time there. He also wrote his highly eccentric column "As I Please" where he expounded about anything that took his interest, ranging from the serious to the light-hearted. At the same time he also wrote for other outlets, including the *Observer*, kept up his occasional Letter to the *Partisan Review*, and did a weekly book review for the *Manchester Evening News*. According to Bernard Crick's biography of Orwell, he published an amazing total of over 100,000 words from the time he left the BBC to January 1945.

Orwell's pay at *Tribune* was decent, £500 per year, and the work not too irksome. Best of all he was required to spend just three days per week at his office, which left him plenty of time to work on his other projects. Orwell was about to enter the most productive and successful phase of his life, a period unfortunately marred by the devastating onslaught of the tuberculosis that would eventually kill him.

Shortly after Orwell went to work at *Tribune*, he and Eileen decided to adopt a child. They had both talked about having children, but he was convinced that he was sterile. Having a child also appealed to him as a way of saying that he believed in the future. It also undermines the image of him as "Gloomy George." He and Eileen were thrilled with the child, whom they adopted in May 1944. They named him Richard after Orwell's father. Unfortunately, less than a year after the adoption, Eileen died while undergoing a hysterectomy.

In the midst of all this, Orwell was completing his first great masterpiece, *Animal Farm*, which he finished in February 1944. It took more than eighteen months for the book to get into print. British publishers were afraid of its implied criticism of a wartime ally, the Soviet Union, and especially its satirical treatment of Stalin. The manuscript was rejected by at least a half-dozen publishing houses in England. Finally, Frederic Warburg published the manuscript in August 1945, just as World War II ended.

The evaluations of *Animal Farm* were inevitably influenced by the politics of the reviewers and their attitude toward Stalinist Russia . . . The Stalinoid Kingsley Martin who'd refused to publish Orwell's reports from Spain, distorted Orwell's political views by claiming that his criticism of the Soviet Union (which in fact began with *The Road to Wigan Pier*) was a recent development. Martin called Orwell a Trotskyist (the derogatory name for anyone who opposed Stalin), claimed that he'd "lost faith in mankind" and concluded that his satire "is historically false and neglectful of the complex truth about Russia."[37]

*Animal Farm* was an immediate success, receiving positive reviews and quickly selling out its first printing of 14,000 copies. Orwell was no longer a talented, if quirky, journalist. The book made him a celebrated and financially comfortable author. This was especially the case when Harcourt, Brace decided to bring out an American edition in 1946.

Orwell had long wanted to leave London for a quieter place. From one of his newest friends, David Astor, the publisher of the *Observer*, he heard about an island in the Hebrides, Jura, which might suit his needs. Now financially set for life he decided to settle there in the spring of 1946. Along with his son and a young housekeeper, Susan Watson, Orwell spent five months on Jura in 1946. He would return again in 1947 and 1948, during which time he wrote his most famous book, *Nineteen Eighty-Four*. The manuscript, which Orwell began in August 1946, was originally titled *The Last Man in Europe*. It went through four drafts before Orwell completed it in late 1948. It would be published under its famous title in June 1949 simultaneously in England and the United States.

*Nineteen Eighty-Four* was an even greater success than *Animal Farm*, and it permanently secured Orwell's status as a major literary figure.

By late 1948 Orwell was seriously ill. His chronic health problems, above all bronchitis and chest colds, had returned toward the end of the war. He had a serious hemorrhage in London in February 1946, which represented the beginning of a series of problems that gradually grew worse. Living in congested, smoggy London and continuing to smoke heavily contributed to the decline of his health. From 1947 until his death in January 1950, Orwell was in and out of sanatoria and hospitals.

Orwell had wanted to remarry after Eileen's death. He proposed to at least four women, often appealing to them on the grounds that they would become the widow of a famous author. In 1949 he asked Sonia Brownell, a former assistant to Cyril Connolly on *Horizon*, to marry him. She agreed and they were married on October 13, 1949 while Orwell was in University College Hospital in London. Three months later, on January 21, 1950, Orwell died of a massive hemorrhage while in hospital. He passed away at the peak of his powers and with numerous literary projects in mind. He was forty-six.

## Chapter 2

# Works

## *Burmese Days*

From his youth Orwell saw himself as a writer. He tells us in his essay "Why I Write" that he had "the lonely child's habit" of making up elaborate stories featuring him in various situations, a phenomenon not uncommon with young people. He also relates that he was fascinated by the very sounds of certain words. Orwell fought this lure of the literary life when he joined the Imperial Police in Burma. But the need to write was such a powerful force in him that he eventually gave in. His dilemma was the choice of what to write.[1]

Orwell tells us that while living in Paris for eighteen months he wrote constantly – short stories, poetry, prose – anything that took his interest. He even made stabs at writing novels. Very little of this material has survived. He did succeed in getting some journalism published before returning to England in late 1929. But at heart he believed that to be a writer one must produce "enormous naturalistic novels with unhappy endings," as he noted in "Why I Write."

31

The 1920s and early 1930s was still the age of the novel in England. Novels, not non-fiction, were bestsellers and a serious writer defined himself by writing fiction not reportage. Orwell's contemporaries (e.g., Graham Greene and Evelyn Waugh) were writing popular novels and establishing a reputation while he remained largely unknown. Orwell sought to make his name in fiction also.

The success of some of his early essays – and especially his study of life on the margin of society, *Down and Out in Paris and London* – did not deter him from his goal to write fiction. One of his problems was that his essays and journalism could draw on his own experiences. In his fiction, until *Animal Farm*, Orwell lacked the imaginative power of those novelists whom he admired, such as James Joyce, D. H. Lawrence, and the more popular Somerset Maugham.[2] All four novels that Orwell produced in the decade of the 1930s had strong autobiographical overtones. By the time he published the last and the best of the lot, *Coming Up for Air* (1939), Orwell probably had exhausted his personal memories as source material and was ready to return to the political journalism at which he excelled.

For a long time Orwell scholars tended to dismiss Orwell's four realistic novels, accepting his own estimate of them as failures of various kinds – he uses terms such as "garbled," "bollix," or "silly potboilers" to describe them. It was typical of Orwell's self-deprecating manner and high literary standards that he would belittle some of his writing – he did it constantly even with brilliant examples of reportage such as "Shooting an Elephant." Recently scholars, such as Loraine Saunders in *The Unsung Artistry of George Orwell* (2008), have begun to see his 1930s novels in a more positive light, approaching them as milestones in his literary development.[3] *Burmese Days*, for example, is highly regarded for its insights into the evils of imperialism in the lives of both the rulers and the ruled. Even *Keep the Aspidistra Flying*, a novel that Orwell later disowned, has found a new audience as a movie. There isn't much to say about *A Clergyman's Daughter* other than it was beyond Orwell's powers as a novelist. *Coming Up for Air*, Orwell's last traditional novel, is treated as comparing favorably with any novel by a major writer in the decade before World War II.

Orwell had begun writing a novel about his experiences in Burma while he was living in Paris. Apparently he hadn't made much progress when he returned to his family's home toward the end of 1929. His major literary effort at that time was writing about his time living with the poor and social outcasts in Paris, which ultimately would lead to his first success, *Down and Out in Paris and London*. At the same time Orwell also was refining his Burmese experiences. As soon as *Down and Out* was accepted for publication in August 1932 by Victor Gollancz's publishing firm, Orwell set about finishing *Burmese Days*.

The setting of *Burmese Days* shows Orwell's debt to W. Somerset Maugham, who wrote so convincingly about the fate of the uprooted English in the East, as well as E. M. Forster's *A Passage to India* which Orwell also admired. *Burmese Days* also pays homage to Kipling, a writer he regarded highly while distrusting his politics. *Burmese Days* is in some respects modeled after Forster's *Passage to India*. While the latter reflects Forster's subtly ironic approach to the evils of imperialism, *Burmese Days* is a bitter and angry attack on the "racket" – one of the favorite words Orwell used to describe the British Empire and all it stood for. The novelist John le Carré would later call *Burmese Days* a perfect "cameo of colonial corruption."[4] It also provided Orwell with an outlet for his anger at the years he wasted as an imperial policeman. Aspects of the novel prefigure Orwell's conviction, most powerfully voiced in "Shooting an Elephant" and "A Hanging," that imperialism corrupted the ruler as much as the ruled.

*Burmese Days* is set sometime after World War I in a timber-rich region of Burma. The novel is filled with long, often lush descriptive passages about the beauty of the Burmese countryside. Descriptive writing with an ability to create a sense of atmosphere is a talent that Orwell also would show in his other novels.

John Flory is the first of Orwell's flawed protagonists. He is a man who believes that his life is a failure and that he is wasting his time in this small Burmese outpost of an empire already showing signs of decline. He not only despises his job as a timber merchant but also hates the people he must associate with in the European Club. Orwell further loads the deck against Flory by having him disfigured by a large dark blue birthmark on his cheek which he seeks to hide from the public.

Flory is living a lie and he knows it. He has a Burmese mistress, Ma Hla May, whom he loathes but continues to exploit, seeing himself as a disgusting fornicator. "Disgusting" is another of Orwell's favorite words in his fiction. Flory has only one friend, an Indian, Dr. Veraswami. Veraswami is a great admirer of all things English – which he views as "modern" in contrast to what he sees as the backwardness of the East. Veraswami's praise for English culture provides Flory with an opportunity to denounce the British Empire as a great swindle. The English, he tells Veraswami, are only in Burma "to steal."

The plot itself is straightforward. An obese, corrupt Burmese magistrate, U Po Kyin, is determined to become the first Asian member of the European Club. He wants to stop Flory from nominating Dr. Veraswami for that honor. To destroy Flory, U Po Kyin plans to use his mistress to denounce him in front of the Europeans.

Flory falls in love with an empty-headed English woman visiting Burma, Elizabeth Lackersteen. He fantasizes that she is a sympathetic, kindred soul. But she is really looking for a husband who can provide her with a comfortable lifestyle. She is disgusted by Flory's egalitarian attitude toward the Burmese, whom she finds "beastly." Flory is blind to her real qualities and proposes marriage – a part of the novel that strains credulity. At first she accepts his proposal. But when his sexual relationship with Ma Hla May becomes public, she withdraws in disgust. At the end of the novel Flory kills himself after also killing his pet dog, Flo – a fitting end for a life based on self-hatred.

The novel is suffused with an atmosphere of failure and deceit. There are virtually no sympathetic characters. Even Dr. Veraswami, Flory's one decent friend, is portrayed as something of a fool with his naïve views of England and the English.

Other characters in the novel are drawn with unredeemed harshness. Elizabeth Lackersteen's mother is a near parody of the memsahib. She finds the native Burmese lazy and insolent, comparing them with the English lower classes. Despite spending years in Burma she cannot speak a word of any Burmese dialect. Ellis, a sharp-tongued member of the European Club, is an example of the blind English racist. He views the Burmese as swine. He is always denouncing the weakness of the authorities, demanding that the Burmese troublemakers should be beaten with whips and have their villages burnt to the ground.

*Burmese Days* is an unrelentingly grim portrait of the British Empire. Years later, in Part II of *The Road to Wigan Pier*, Orwell would write of his time as a Burma policeman that he "hated the imperialism I was serving with a bitterness which I probably cannot make clear."[5] Other than affection for the beauties of the Burmese countryside there is virtually nothing in the novel but pettiness, corruption, and vileness. Even the Burmese are portrayed harshly – there is no romanticizing the native in Orwell's eyes, a theme which will appear later in his powerful essay, "Shooting an Elephant." The novel nevertheless packs a punch. Even if the characters are cardboard, the atmosphere is vividly conveyed, and the author's anger toward the corruption of the British Empire comes across as real.

*Burmese Days* also exemplifies Orwell's emerging literary skills. While the dialogue is often stilted and artificial, the story moves quickly and the atmospherics are well handled. Some of the set pieces (such as Flory's hunting expedition with Elizabeth, Flory's discussions with Dr. Veraswami about the relative values of English culture) are brilliantly portrayed. Orwell's anger at the racism implicit in the British Empire is apparent throughout, though the impact of this anger is less effectively developed than in his two anti-imperialist essays. Orwell was almost too angry in *Burmese Days*, something he recognized when he later remarked to a friend that it was a queer experience, like reading a novel by a stranger. (Yet unlike some of his other work, he came to appreciate *Burmese Days* and wanted to see it reprinted.)

Orwell sensed that *Burmese Days* was flawed. In his typical self-deprecating manner, he told his girlfriend, Brenda Salkeld, that writing *Burmese Days* "depresses me horribly." When he completed the novel he was surprised that his agent, Leonard Moore, was enthusiastic about it. Personally he told Moore he was "sick of the sight of it."[6]

> Flory's fall is the result of his transgressions among the Burmese – who he has failed to embrace warmly enough for a real break from injustice. His half-hearted, "half-educated" rebellion brings him only woe. It proves to be too little and too late to redeem him.
> Either resist effectively, or do not resist at all. This is Orwell's implicit message upon leaving Burma.[7]

Gollancz, who was pleased with Orwell's success with *Down and Out*, was reluctant to publish *Burmese Days*. He feared that the setting, incidents, and especially the names of the characters might open him to a libel suit. Eventually Moore was able to place *Burmese Days* with the American firm Harper & Company, who published it in October 1934. *Burmese Days* sold surprisingly well, going into a second printing and selling around 3,000 copies according to an estimate by the Orwell scholar Peter Davison. A year later, seeing no lawsuits, Gollancz decided to bring out an English edition.[8]

Gollancz had Orwell make a number of changes in names and local settings so as to avoid the strict English libel laws. Orwell admitted to Norman Collins, one of the directors of Gollancz's firm, that the novel was indeed based on fact. Orwell even went through the list of names of people serving in the Indian Civil Service to make sure there was none similar to the characters in *Burmese Days*. All of this tampering with the novel infuriated him and convinced him that the finished work would be a failure – "garbled" in his words.

*Burmese Days* was a modest success when it appeared in England. It sold out its first printing of 2,500 copies and Gollancz brought out a second printing – good signs for a first novel. Coming as it did so soon after the success of *Down and Out* it helped solidify Orwell's reputation as an author to watch. In May 1944 Penguin brought out a cheap, 9d, edition which sold around 60,000 copies, a remarkable figure given that Orwell's fame for *Animal Farm* was still a year away.[9]

## A Clergyman's Daughter

Orwell's success with *Burmese Days* encouraged him to try another novel. In fact, while he was ironing out the details of *Burmese Days*, in the spring of 1934 he began developing a new novel. Orwell was a compulsive writer. He had always to be writing or he felt he had wasted his time. It is amazing how prolific he was given his need to hold down part-time jobs while writing almost full-time.

Orwell's new novel, *A Clergyman's Daughter*, was by far his poorest effort and one of his greatest failures. It would eventually be named by him as one of his books that he didn't want reprinted. In some ways it was an experiment, fueled by Orwell's reading of and admiration for James Joyce's *Ulysses*.[10]

It is difficult to know what inspired Orwell to make his protagonist, Dorothy Hare, an unmarried woman. It is true that one of the women that he was romantically interested in at the time he was writing *A Clergyman's Daughter*, Brenda Salkeld, was in fact a vicar's daughter. But Orwell had little intimate knowledge of women at this stage in his life. As a result, one of the main flaws in the novel itself was Orwell's inability to enter the mind of a female character. Some commentators believe that Orwell was inspired by the work of another writer he admired, D. H. Lawrence's "The Daughter of the Vicar." Another possible inspiration for his new novel comes from a scene in *Down and Out* that Orwell mentioned stayed with him. A clergyman and his daughter, Orwell wrote, were watching him and his fellow tramps "as though we were aquarium fishes."

Orwell also was trying something new in the novel. He is both the narrator of the story, commenting from the outside, and Dorothy herself, ruminating about her condition. It was a feat that great novelists could carry off, but it was beyond Orwell's powers at this stage in his literary development.

*A Clergyman's Daughter* consists of five chapters. One of the flaws in the novel is the fact that the chapters lack a true connecting structure. They read like independent sketches loosely linked.

Dorothy Hare's father is a vicar who has lost interest in his church and his profession. His wife is dead and Dorothy, now twenty-eight, has taken over the role that her mother performed with the congregation. Her father is cold and aloof with her. Dorothy, the protagonist of the novel, is plain-looking, has no social life and suffers from low self-esteem. She can't conceive of any kind of life beyond what she has. Orwell's portrait of her is unsympathetic, making it difficult for the reader to identify with her or even her plight.

Orwell also makes her sexually frustrated. She only has one male friend, a middle-aged, semi-roué, Mr. Warburton, who serves to stand for everything Dorothy is not. (Warburton is never given a first name.) He is worldly, financially well-off, but most importantly he is romantically interested in her. While she finds him attractive, the thought of sex with "horrible furry beasts," as she describes men, disgusts her.

The first chapter is one day in Dorothy's life which emphasizes how boring and meaningless her existence is as she goes about the tasks of a vicar's surrogate wife. To get the story moving and Dorothy out of the house, Orwell has Mr. Warburton try to seduce her, which brings on a bout of amnesia. The scene lacks all sense of believability. Dorothy finds herself wandering the countryside and in a series of three chapters she falls in with tramps hop picking, spends a night with the desperately poor in Trafalgar Square, and gets a job teaching at an appalling school. All three chapters draw on Orwell's own life and are little more than attempts at fictionalizing his own experiences. He might have been able to carry this effort off if the protagonist was male. But his Dorothy in these situations seems unreal.

The hop picking material is derived from a diary Orwell kept when he was gathering material for one of his articles on the downtrodden and would have fit *Down and Out* better than any novel. The Trafalgar Square scene is done in dialogue and owes its inspiration to the "Ulysses in Nighttown" sequence in Joyce's novel which profoundly impressed Orwell.[11] He found Joyce inspiring and demoralizing – reading Joyce, he wrote, made him want to throw up his own writing. Orwell would come to view *A Clergyman's Daughter* in his own words as "tripe." But he told the French translator of the novel that he was proud of the Trafalgar Square scene. The school section also is derived from Orwell's time teaching in two ghastly for-profit educational institutions.

After putting Dorothy through these harrowing experiences, Orwell has her rescued and brought home by Mr. Warburton. Again he proposes marriage. Dorothy rejects him in order to resume her life with her father. The ending is disappointing. Dorothy returns to her former life but now has lost the faith that had sustained her at the beginning of the novel. Now she is sustained by a kind of "religiousless Christianity."

*A Clergyman's Daughter* was a failed experiment, one that Orwell admitted left him frustrated. It is difficult to understand why he chose a theme that was intimately connected to religion given his own negative views of Christianity and religion in general. It was difficult enough to try to enter a young woman's mind but especially so that of a woman in a religious milieu.

Orwell knew what he wanted to do with the novel but couldn't make it work. As with almost everything Orwell wrote, it had a political component and was an indictment of the capitalist class system and the debilitating impact of poverty especially on unmarried women. But unlike *Down and Out*, it doesn't convey the message in a believable way. The characters were caricatures – feeble imitations of Dickens. Dorothy never seems real, while Warburton comes across like a third-rate H. G. Wells with his worldly philosophizing. Another female character, Mrs. Creevy, who runs the school where Dorothy teaches, like Mrs. Lackersteen in *Burmese Days*, is a grotesque caricature of a certain kind of middle-class woman. Dorothy, herself, has enraged some feminist critics who find her a "pathetic drudge." No wonder feminist scholars have accused Orwell of being a misogynist.[12]

Orwell finished *A Clergyman's Daughter* in October 1934. He had little optimism about its future. When he sent it to Moore, Orwell told him that he had "made a muck of it."[13] Orwell was surprised when Moore thought it publishable. Moore sent it to Gollancz who had it vetted for libel. Gollancz's reader recommended publication, calling the novel "very original" – so much for his editorial judgment.

*A Clergyman's Daughter* was published in March 1935 – they turned around novels quickly in those days. With *Burmese Days* coming out in England two months later, Orwell had two novels published almost at the same time – a remarkable feat and a testament to his commitment to authorship. The reviews were a mixed bag.[14] To Orwell it was a "silly potboiler" which made him want to "spew." Despite that, he told Brenda Salkeld that there were some decent passages in it, probably referring to his takeoff on Joyce in the Trafalgar Square scene.

The "potboiler" sold surprisingly well. Around 2,000 copies were printed and none was remaindered. Soon after completing *A Clergyman's Daughter* Orwell moved to London to work in a bookshop. By the time *A Clergyman's Daughter* was published he had already begun his next novel.

> [T]he special failure of *A Clergyman's Daughter* is, I believe the result of Orwell's willful evasion. He must remain on guard not to enter a female world view. When the novel first appeared, critics frequently referred to Dorothy Hare's "breakdown," the incident ostensibly accounting for her loss of memory and subsequent descent into another social class. But Dorothy does not suffer a breakdown; she suffers from a creator, Orwell, who having invented a female protagonist, does not know how to get her out of the house and into the street . . . As it happens, what is most notable about Dorothy, in contrast to Orwell's other protagonists, is the extent to which Orwell molds her into a cipher.[15]

## Keep the Aspidistra Flying

Orwell's next novel, like his previous pair, drew directly on his own experiences. Written in 1935 while working at Booklover's Corner, which was owned by a pair of mild radicals and followers of the Esperanto movement, the Westropes, *Keep the Aspidistra Flying* was Orwell's next attempt to write a realistic or naturalistic work of fiction. He continued to think of himself primarily as a novelist. While he had certain radical notions – one of his associates at this time described him as a Tory anarchist – to Orwell, being a writer still meant producing great works of imaginative literature not political tracts. He remained under the thrall of Joyce and D. H. Lawrence.

The protagonist of his new novel, Gordon Comstock (there is no evidence that Orwell knew of the infamous American censor of literature, Anthony Comstock, who had died in 1915 when Orwell was twelve years old), also is more closely modeled on Orwell than John Flory – Peter Davison describes Gordon as "a failed Orwell."[16] Many of Comstock's pet peeves are those of Orwell at this time in his life – the corruption of capitalism, the evils of materialism, lack of money, the sheer drudgery of working in a bookstore, a writer's need for privacy, etc. Orwell puts in Comstock's mouth his own anger and frustration at trying to make a living as a writer. And yet by the time he wrote *Keep the Aspidistra Flying*, Orwell already had three books in print plus articles and reviews for English journals such as *Adelphi*, the *New England Weekly*, the *New Statesman*, and *Time and Tide*. He may not have made much money yet at writing, but he was becoming known in certain literary circles as a man to watch. Gollancz, no mean judge of financial possibilities if not literary skills, thought that Orwell had a future and was worth cultivating.[17]

*Keep the Aspidistra Flying*, like *A Clergyman's Daughter*, has a circular quality to it. Comstock goes full circle with his life. He is determined (like Orwell) to be a serious writer. He quits his job writing advertising copy, which he has a talent for, at the New Albion Publicity Company to produce a great epic poem about the city of London, undergoes a series of adventures, and ends up back at the advertising agency. *Keep the Aspidistra Flying* also owes a debt to one of the novelists that Orwell admired and championed, George Gissing. Like Gissing, Orwell was fascinated by those on the margins of society, especially the struggling lower middle classes who were the clerks, bookkeepers, and accountants struggling to make a living in the grinding capitalist system of their times.

What makes Comstock such a fascinating character is the qualities that Orwell gives him. He is constantly railing against what he calls "the Money God" and believes that society's materialism keeps him from being recognized for his poetry. He has published a small collection of verse, appropriately entitled "Mice," which fails to sell and is remaindered – a constant reminder of Comstock's literary failures.

Comstock's family is shocked when he quits his job at the advertising agency to become a writer. They had done everything to see that he got a superior education that would enable him to redeem the family that had fallen on hard times. The connection with Orwell's family's reaction to his leaving the Imperial Police is obvious.

Comstock has only three friends. His sister Julia, who runs a teashop, is clearly modeled after Orwell's sister Avril. Philip Ravelston, the rich, leftwing owner of the socialist journal *AntiChrist*, who Comstock argues with about politics but whom he also sponges off, resembles Sir Richard Rees physically as well as in his politics and in his position with the journal *Adelphi*. Orwell portrays Ravelston as guilt ridden by his riches, trying unsuccessfully to identify with the working classes. Ravelston is a genuine friend who encourages Comstock in his epic poem, "London Pleasures," which is never completed. He even secretly arranges for some of Comstock's poetry to be published.

By far the most important character in the novel other than the protagonist is Rosemary Waterlow, Comstock's girlfriend. She works at the New Albion with Comstock and loves him despite his flaws. She is not fully drawn, but is the most human character in the novel. A theme of the novel is Comstock's attempt to have sex with her, but to be constantly frustrated by his lack of privacy – his landlady, another grim Dickensian character, Mrs. Wisbeach will not let him have women in his rooms.

In one scene Comstock takes Rosemary out for a day in the country. What starts out as a pleasant excursion turns into a nightmare. Comstock spends all his money on a meal at an expensive hotel and when he tries to seduce Rosemary she spurns him because he doesn't have a condom.

Comstock's life is a constant failure. His epic poem never develops because he can't find the time to work on it. After receiving a sudden windfall of £10 when an American journal buys one of his poems, Comstock goes on a spree. He takes Ravelston and Rosemary to an expensive restaurant where he proceeds to get drunk. After Rosemary leaves them, Comstock takes Ravelston to some seedy pubs where they pick up a pair of prostitutes, one of whom robs Comstock of £5. Comstock ends up in jail for his drunken behavior, which enables Orwell to work in some grim detail from his own time in jail – the filthy condition of the cell, the smelly, filled chamber pot, etc.

Comstock is forced to take a series of dead-end jobs working in run-down bookstores, which enables Orwell to voice some of his views on such stores and their customers.

The novel's dénouement takes place when Rosemary visits him in his dirty room and allows him to make love to her. Orwell portrays the scene as joyless and unsatisfying. Later Rosemary tells Comstock that she is pregnant. Despite all his railings against the system and his disgust at middle-class morality, he decides to marry her and return to the New Albion.

The character of Rosemary has offended some feminists who find her unreal and entirely too submissive. Feminists also find the ending disturbing, seeing it as a masculine view of how women trap men by getting pregnant.[18] Rosemary is by far the most likeable of the female characters in Orwell's novels. Perhaps this has something to do with the fact that as he was writing the novel he met and fell in love with his future wife, Eileen O'Shaughnessy. His romance with Eileen might have softened the way that Orwell portrays Rosemary's role in Gordon's life.

Gordon and Rosemary end up in a nice flat off the Edgware Road with Gordon earning £4 a week writing advertising copy about a new product to reduce foot odor. In the window of their flat they have an aspidistra plant, a symbol of middle-class respectability and a sign that life goes on: "Well, once again things were happening in the Comstock family."[19]

Orwell completed *Keep the Aspidistra Flying* by January 1936, just as he was ready to leave on his visit to Wigan Pier for research on his study of poverty and unemployment in the north of England. Gollancz had his usual worries about a new book and while Orwell was gathering research material he had to deal with the potential libel issues. In particular, Gollancz was concerned that the New Albion Company and some of the slogans that Gordon devised might be libelous. Orwell became angry at the pettiness of some of the changes demanded and at one point told Gollancz that they "utterly ruined the book."[20] But he was careful to say that he would still like to see the book published.

*Keep the Aspidistra Flying* appeared on April 20, 1936, a little over three months after Orwell turned the manuscript over to Gollancz – remarkable in itself and an indication of what Gollancz thought of Orwell. Unlike his previous books, Moore was unable to interest any American publisher in the new novel – its atmosphere was too overpoweringly negative. They also found the story and theme too English for American audiences. It would not appear in the United States until after Orwell's death.

*Keep the Aspidistra Flying* received mixed reviews. Compton Mackenzie, Richard Church, and Orwell's friend Rees gave it a positive send off. Cyril Connolly reviewed it twice. In the influential *New Statesman*, Connolly noted that in *Burmese Days* Orwell loved the countryside and that showed through in his vivid descriptions, while in *Keep the Aspidistra Flying* he appeared to hate London and everything it stood for. Connolly compared reading the new novel to sitting in a dentist's chair.

*Keep the Aspidistra Flying* sold approximately 2,500 copies, which made it the least successful of his books. He thought the novel a failure, dismissing it (along with *A Clergyman's Daughter*) as "a silly potboiler" in some notes he left for his literary executor in 1945.

*Keep the Aspidistra Flying* is better than that. Despite the novel's flaws it shows Orwell's growing literary powers. Gordon Comstock is an unforgettable character, much more real than John Flory or Dorothy Hare. It is true that his tirades are often tiresome, but they have a certain authenticity about them. It is interesting that this novel, more than any other work that Orwell wrote in the 1930s, would influence a generation of English writers in the years after World War II. The "Angry Young Men" of the 1950s owe a great debt to Orwell, as authors as different as Kingsley Amis, John Osborne, and John Wain would admit. After all, Jimmy Porter in *Look Back in Anger* or Amis's anti-hero in *Lucky Jim* sounds just like Gordon Comstock in his complaints about the unfairness of society and the people who control your lives.[21]

## Coming Up for Air

More than two years passed between the publication of *Keep the Aspidistra Flying* and the appearance of Orwell's fourth and last traditional novel, *Coming Up for Air*, in June 1939. In those two years Orwell's life had undergone a major transformation. He had married Eileen O'Shaughnessy, who brought a degree of normality to his life and more importantly was a staunch supporter of his literary aspirations. He published his greatest success, and the book that brought him to national attention, *The Road to Wigan Pier* (1937). It called attention to his singular talent for skilled sociological journalism. In 1937–38, Orwell's involvement in the Spanish Civil War gave rise to another example of brilliant reportage, *Homage to Catalonia* (1938), which while not a financial success, at the very least, furthered his reputation as a writer with a unique talent for reportage and journalism. By the time Orwell began working on his new novel he had matured as a writer. He had developed his unique "voice," that clear, direct style without artifice which reached fruition in *Homage to Catalonia* as well as in such powerful essays as "A Hanging" and "Shooting an Elephant." By the late 1930s Orwell had shown the ability to write important non-fiction and had honed the literary style that would characterize his prose for the rest of his life. But he still was drawn to the novel format, believing that this was one literary skill he hadn't fully mastered.

In December 1937, while in the midst of negotiations over the publication of his book on the Spanish war, Orwell told his agent, Leonard Moore, that he had a new work of fiction in mind – he had even chosen a title – *Coming Up for Air*.[22] It was to be an examination of a man trying to escape his boring existence and family responsibilities by returning to the village of his youth. Once again, Orwell had barely finished one book before he was outlining another – the sign of a truly driven writer.

Before he could begin work on his new novel, Orwell was taken ill with a bout of tuberculosis, possibly a result of his time at the front in Spain as well as the general lack of care he took with his health. He spent the best part of 1938 (March to September) in a sanatorium in Kent. While not allowed to do any writing during his recovery, he continued outlining his new novel.

Orwell's doctors recommended a long rest in a warm climate, something which was out of the question given his financial situation. The novelist L. H. Myers, an admirer of Orwell's writings, arranged anonymously to advance him £300. This was a significant sum for those days.[23] (For some idea of modern purchasing power, that figure should be multiplied by a factor of 40 or 50.) Orwell accepted the money on the understanding that it was a loan to be paid back and not a gift. When he became financially secure he made sure to repay the loan.

With the money Orwell and his wife traveled to Marrakech in Morocco in September 1938, where they stayed for seven months. He started writing *Coming Up for Air* in September and completed it five months later in January 1939. It was his last and, in many ways, the best and most sophisticated of his traditional novels.

Continuing his experimentation with writing, Orwell composed *Coming Up for Air* in the first person, which gives the narrative a denser quality than his other novels. Using the first-person narrative technique enabled Orwell to make long, detailed digressions through his main character on topics of the day that interested him such as the loss of community, the coming of war, etc. Later he would note that no one had observed that he did not use a semi-colon throughout the novel.

*Coming Up for Air* is Orwell's most nostalgic novel. It is the story of George Bowling, a fat, 45-year-old, lower-middle-class insurance salesman who is experiencing a mid-life crisis. He is Orwell's most likeable protagonist with all the pet quirks and phobias of his author. In some ways he resembles Leopold Bloom, the protagonist of Joyce's *Ulysses*, another average man in crisis. Jeffrey Meyers calls Bowling Orwell's "most engaging hero."[24] He may not be a "hero" but he is certainly preferable to the morbid Flory, the quiescent Dorothy Hare, or the often irritating Gordon Comstock. Best of all, there is something very human about Bowling.

Like his other protagonists, Bowling has a great deal of Orwell in him, even the same first name. Again like his author, Bowling is something of a grumpy Tory anarchist, the very words used to describe Orwell at this time in his life by his friend Cyril Connolly. Bowling loves the years of his youth. "Nineteen thirteen," he says at one point – the world will never again be what it was in that wonderful year. Physically Bowling doesn't resemble the gaunt Orwell, but does remark at one point in the novel that every fat man has a thin man inside him struggling to get out.

Bowling was born in 1893, which enables him to undergo experiences that Orwell missed. He grew up in the years before World War I, a time Orwell believed was England's last golden age – a theme he returned to again and again in his writings. Bowling also served in World War I and was even wounded, for which he received a small pension. Orwell believed that those like him too young to serve in the war sensed that they had missed something important in life.

Bowling is married to another of the female shrews that Orwell was so effective at delineating and who dotted his fiction. His wife, Hilda, in many ways is Elizabeth Lackersteen grown fat and ugly – "the fly in the milk jug," as Bowling describes her.[25] She is a constant nag about money matters, a theme that Orwell associated with the middle-class fear that they were one step from falling into the ranks of the working classes. Bowling has two children who hardly appear in the novel except to represent another way in which marriage has trapped him.

Like his other novels, *Coming Up for Air* is circular in structure. It takes Bowling from his home in a modern, stultifying suburb west of London on a journey back to his youthful home in the village of Lower Binfield. But in the course of the journey Bowling is disappointed by what he finds, discovering that truly you can't go home again. He eventually returns to Hilda and the children a disillusioned man.

Orwell launches the novel by having Bowling win £50 on a horse race and decide to undertake a trip down memory lane without telling his wife. The novel opens with Bowling just getting his first set of false teeth, further setting the stage for his growing awareness that time has passed him by. His adventure is a desperate attempt to flee into the past he affectionately remembers and try to recapture his lost youth.

Orwell uses the novel, and especially the character of George Bowling, as the voice for all the issues that obsessed him at this time in his life. He has Bowling and Hilda attend a Left Book Club meeting where the speaker spews a message of hatred no different than any fascist demagogue. The socialists and communists, Orwell seems to be saying, are no different from the fascists. This scene enables Orwell to get some payback at the leftwing Victor Gollancz for rejecting *Homage to Catalonia* sight unseen.

By the late 1930s, Orwell was deeply disillusioned by world events, especially by what was happening in Spain where the fascist forces were near victory. Running through *Coming Up for Air* is a sense of nervous tension that a war was coming and that it would be more awful than anyone imagined. At the time he wrote *Coming Up for Air*, Orwell was associated with the Independent Labour Party, which held that there was essentially no difference between capitalist England and Nazi Germany. Both nations were expressions of different forms of capitalist degeneration. Orwell's anger and frustration feed *Coming Up for Air*.

Although some commentators have labeled *Coming Up for Air* non-political, there is a definite political undertone running through the novel. Orwell believed that the long era of peace that England slumbered through was about to end. The war that was coming would be different. Hitler and Stalin, he has Bowling think, aren't like past rulers. "They're after something quite new – something never heard of before."[26] In one of the last scenes in the novel English planes accidently drop bombs on Lower Binfield, foreshadowing what is about to happen.

Bowling, like Orwell, is disgusted at the modern world with its spirit-killing materialism. When Bowling returns to Lower Binfield he finds everything has changed, and not for the better. Lower Binfield is no longer a village of people who, whatever their faults, cared for each other, but has turned into a factory town making armaments and munitions. This leads Orwell into a digression on the coming war, a theme he first touched on in *Keep the Aspidistra Flying* and the end of *Homage to Catalonia* where he speaks of the English sleeping the deep sleep of peace with war in the offing.

Bowling learns that you truly can't go home again. He looks up his first love and finds that she has turned into an ugly woman. He visits one of his old teachers, Mr. Porteus, whom he had admired for his wisdom, and finds that he is unaware of what is happening in the real world. The fishing pond that Bowling dreamed about, he discovers is now polluted and filled with rubber tires and rusted bicycle parts, the trash of modern civilization.

Bowling returns home to find Hilda accusing him of going off to have an affair. He denies it but finally resigns himself to the fact that no matter what he says or does, she won't believe him. Like Dorothy Hare and Gordon Comstock (though not John Flory), Bowling resigns himself to his fate and waits calmly for the bombs to begin to fall.

In March 1939, Orwell returned from Morocco and delivered the manuscript to Gollancz. Libel issues were insignificant compared to Orwell's previous novels and *Coming Up for Air* was published on June 12.

*Coming Up for Air* was certainly Orwell's most sophisticated novel of the 1930s. It was clearly written, often witty, the story unfolded logically and the main characters, especially Bowling, were carefully developed. The novel sold almost 3,000 copies. It might have gone on to become Orwell's first fictional bestseller, but it appeared just as Europe began its drift to war. Orwell certainly thought highly of it. When Secker & Warburg wanted to bring out a uniform edition of his works in 1948, he recommended *Coming Up for Air* as their first choice. *Burmese Days* was his second choice, which tells you how he ranked his four realistic novels. He didn't mention *A Clergyman's Daughter* or *Keep the Aspidistra Flying*.

Some critics believe that writing traditional fiction represented a false start for Orwell. Recently there is a renewed interest in his four novels of the 1930s. The English scholar Loraine Saunders in a recent study of these novels has found what she labels an "unsung artistry" in them.[27] They certainly are worth a read.

> *Coming Up for Air* is undoubtedly Orwell's most recognizably proletarian novel, . . . It is also Orwell's most propagandist . . . Orwell is writing this novel with World War Two looming and fascist dictatorships gaining more and more ground in Europe. Orwell understood that it was largely through middle-class support, by promising economic stability, that Hitler, Mussolini and Franco were successful.[28]

## Down and Out in Paris and London

During the time when Orwell struggled to become a recognized novelist, he also began to develop the skills of a first-class writer of crisp documentary prose. Although for a long time he saw himself as an author of traditional fiction, the sphere of elite journalism and reportage witnessed his initial breakthrough as a writer.

During the eighteen months Orwell spent in Paris he wrote copiously in all literary forms. He produced two (possibly three) novels, some short stories, poetry, as well as numerous other pieces of writing that he destroyed as worthless, an action that he later came to regret.

Orwell arrived back in England in December 1929 with little to show for his literary endeavors. His publications were few, just a couple of small pieces for minor newspapers and magazines in Paris and London. These pieces were pedestrian and gave little hint of his later skills. In fact, all his efforts at becoming a writer had earned Orwell the grand sum of £20. His family, especially his father, was not reconciled to his desire to be a writer. Orwell, however, was encouraged because a leading English intellectual journal, *Adelphi*, had accepted his story "The Spike" for publication.

On this slim basis Orwell continued his pursuit of literary success. He was working on a number of projects while doing various odd jobs to make a living – serving as a companion to two young boys, teaching at two schools, working in a bookshop. He also continued investigating the world of the destitute and poor in England and took up traveling around with tramps and the unemployed in order to gain an insight into the netherworld of the desperate and the down and out.

While in Paris he had already produced drafts of what would later become *Burmese Days*, and his breakthrough documentary, *Down and Out in Paris and London*. He continued working on both projects while waiting for *Adelphi* to publish "The Spike." The editor, Max Plowman, gave him the opportunity to do some reviews for the journal, and in 1930 and early 1931 Orwell wrote four book reviews, his first serious publications for a respectable journal. Brief yet insightful, they show a command of the art of reviewing and a lack of fear in making judgments, attributes that would typify Orwell's mature writing. A review of Lewis Mumford's biography of Herman Melville, for instance, already reveals Orwell's gift for vivid imagery. Accusing Mumford of over-interpreting Melville's poetry, Orwell compared it to "eating an apple for the pips."[29]

Orwell's political and economic views were still unformed at this time. He was critical of capitalism but as yet had not developed a coherent political philosophy. In many ways his political and social views resembled those of nineteenth-century Tory radicals such as William Cobbett or William Hazlitt – angry at society without a clear idea of what to do. Charles Dickens's influence on this thinking also was strongly apparent. Orwell was incensed at the conditions under which the poor lived. At the time, Orwell resembled nothing more than a Tory anarchist, a term often used to describe him.

In October 1930, he sent a short version of his Paris experiences entitled *A Scullion's Diary* to the English publishing house Jonathan Cape. At 30,000 to 35,000 words it was too short for publication and Cape rejected it. Orwell then reworked the manuscript by incorporating his English experiences of tramping and living among the desperately poor, some material from "The Spike," and an essay, later published in the *New Statesman* ("Clink").

The revised manuscript was reshaped in 1931 and resubmitted to Cape, which rejected it a second time. In December 1931, T. S. Eliot at Faber and Faber also rejected it, although Eliot, at least, was mildly encouraging, saying that "we did find it of very great interest."[30]

Orwell was ready to give up on the manuscript. He told one of his friends, Mabel Fierz, to destroy it. Instead she took it to Leonard Moore, who thought it had literary merit. He took it to Victor Gollancz, who in 1928 had founded a leftwing publishing firm. Gollancz was interested in books critical of the failures of capitalism and saw possibilities in Orwell's critique of its evils in Paris and London. In August 1932, Gollancz agreed to publish the book, giving Orwell an advance of £40.

There were two problems with the manuscript – what to title it and the fact that Orwell wanted it published anonymously because he believed its sordid tales would shame his family. A number of titles were considered including Orwell's choice, *Lady Poverty*. Eventually Gollancz chose *Down and Out in Paris and London*. Eager for the book to see print, Orwell reluctantly accepted this title.

Orwell considered a number of pseudonyms: P. S. Burton, Kenneth Miles, H. Lewis Allways. Finally he decided on "George Orwell." It is difficult to imagine this great English twentieth-century writer with the name H. Lewis Allways.

"George Orwell" was launched, although he would continue to write under the name Eric Blair for another couple of years and use the two names depending on how and when he knew the person he was writing to.

*Down and Out* was published on January 9, 1933 in London and six months later by Harper Brothers in the United States. The reviews were largely positive in both countries and sales were good for a book by an unknown writer. In England, the first edition sold out, as did a smaller second run. Approximately 3,000 copies were sold, a solid beginning – and one that indicated to Gollancz that he had a potentially successful author on his hands.

*Down and Out* is divided into two roughly equal sections. The first part set in Paris covers just a few weeks in Orwell's life. The conceit is that he found himself temporarily broke – he claimed that he lost his money. He later told friends that a prostitute robbed him – and thus was forced into the ranks of the destitute. In fact, his aunt and her husband lived nearby and could have bailed him out of his financial distress at any time.

Orwell's portrait of Paris is picaresque – a focus on the seamier side of the city's life and peopled with characters right out of a Zola novel.

When *Down and Out* appeared, people didn't know what to make of it. Was it an autobiography? Pure fiction? A blend of the two? Orwell later wrote that everything he described did take place at one time or another. Michael Shelden in his biography labels the final work a "border zone between fact and fiction," a comment which seems right on the mark.

We now know that many of the incidents in the book that have been questioned really took place. In 1989 an annotated presentation copy of *Down and Out* surfaced that Orwell had given to his girlfriend, Brenda Salkeld. Orwell's contemporary notes verified some of the more unbelievable scenes in the book. In the introduction to the French edition, he wrote that he often combined incidents, rearranged events etc. for effect. Of his gallery of misfits and eccentrics, for instance, the incredible character named Boris was real. Orwell used Boris (as he would use Bozo, the pavement artist, in the London half of the book) as the main character through which to highlight the book's themes. Because Boris and Bozo are the only fully developed figures in the book, the reader gets a sense that they were based on real people and not entirely fictional creations. In *Down and Out* Orwell is fully present and several dramatic turns of event befall him, but we see these events through the other characters in the book who also are victims.

Boris, a White Russian émigré, is a wonderful portrait with his unbounded enthusiasm and optimism, quoting Marshal Foch when things are going badly, always "Attaquez, Attaquez, Attaquez." Orwell told Salkeld that he was a real character. In fact, Orwell builds the first half of the book around his adventures with Boris. Orwell's own first-person character is kind of a hanger-on, even an observer, throughout this journey into the lower depths.

One remarkable scene features Boris admonishing Orwell for being a writer. Writing is "bosh" Boris says. If you must write, he says, then write to your mistress asking for money. The advice is amusing and ironic, especially given that Orwell had done everything he could for the past few years to become a writer – given up a steady job in the Imperial Police, lived in poverty in France and England, alienated his family – and still had little to show for it all.

There is a certain inconsistency in the Paris section, a result of trying to tie together an unconnected series of bizarre vignettes, partly borne of the fact that Orwell is not an investigator of the world of poverty, but rather an observer who could escape anytime he wanted. Some of the best vignettes are unforgettable and crafted with signs of literary skills for which he would later become famous. For example, the opening description of his hotel and the street on which he lives possesses a directness and clarity that gives the reader a real feel for his Paris slum.

"The rue du Coq d'Or, Paris, seven in the morning. A succession of furious, choking yells from the street. Madame Monce, who kept the little hotel opposite mine, had come out on to the pavement to address a lodger on the third floor. Her bare feet were stuck into sabots and her grey hair was streaming down."[31] "Bare feet" in "sabots" is an unforgettable image. For a first book, Orwell was showing signs of the talent that characterizes his later writings – vivid descriptions and sharp, clear images.

Orwell would use the same technique in the opening of *The Road to Wigan Pier* – using physical description to place the reader in the scene.

Orwell had a gift for describing dirt and filth, and he paints an unforgettable picture of his room infested with bugs. "Near the ceiling, long lines of bugs marched all day like columns of soldiers, and at night came down ravenously hungry, so that one had to get up every few hours and kill them in hecatombs."[32] Comparing the bed bugs to "columns of soldiers" and use of the term "hecatombs" shows that Orwell was developing a keen eye for vivid detail.

One of the chapters, the retelling of the life of "Charlie," a wealthy young man who relates a preposterous tale of debauching and raping a young woman in a red-lined underground chamber, sounds like something out of a bad nineteenth-century novel. There is no note in his annotation that this tale was true. Another story tells of a miser who gets swindled in a deal for cocaine. The cocaine turned out to be face powder and the miser literally dies of a broken heart at the loss of his money. The villains in this tale are Jews; likewise Boris is forever denouncing Jews, and those Jews who appear in *Down and Out* are portrayed harshly. All this raises the uncomfortable issue of Orwell's anti-Semitism at the time.

In this regard Orwell was typical of his class and his time. Most British people in the 1920s and 1930s offhandedly viewed Jews in stereotypical ways. One has only to look at the novels of contemporaries such as Evelyn Waugh or Graham Greene to confirm this. Orwell was no better or worse than his peers. Unlike many of them, however, he overcame much of this reflexive anti-Semitism after World War II and the Holocaust.

The centerpiece of the first part of *Down and Out* occurs when the desperate Orwell has to resort to working as a *plongeur* (dishwasher) in a Paris hotel restaurant. It was typical of Orwell that he would choose the lowest and most disgusting of occupations for himself. His description of the kitchen's awful heat, the slimy floor, the excruciating noise, overwhelming dirt, and bread-bin filled with cockroaches – all of this separated from the fine restaurant by a mere glass door – has become legendary. Orwell's keen eye focused on the distinctions in the hotel, between the waiters and the cooks, between the patron and the clients, while everywhere in the service quarters "dirt festered – a secret vein of dirt, running through the great garish hotel like the intestines through a man's body." Orwell was always good at distinctions. It had something to do with his fascination with class conception that he grew up with.

The second half of *Down and Out* focuses on Orwell's experiences with tramps and tramping. When he returned from Burma he had started tramping, perhaps as a way of purging himself of what he had done in the name of the British Empire. The material he accumulated on his various expeditions formed the heart of the London half of the book.

The conceit in the second part is that Orwell had a job waiting for him but it would it would be a month before it began. Thus with little money he had to live on the margins of society. Again this was not true. Orwell had many friends and family in England to whom he could have turned if he had needed help.

Part II possesses greater coherence than the Paris section and reads like a flowing tale, but it lacks the vividness, the sharp detail, and the unbuttoned hilarity of life amid poverty in France. Orwell is keen as ever to note class distinctions. For example, he points out that in England clothes are powerful things. When he dresses like a tramp, he enters a new world and is treated differently by everyone. To the tramps, he is one of them despite his accent; to the rest of society, he is either a potential menace or invisible.

> The two sections do not, indeed, fit together as a narrative and neither is it all of a piece stylistically. The Paris half has passages both of purple literary Blair and of plain-style Orwell. The London passages both hang together better and are plain style throughout.[33]

Orwell also stressed the differences between London and Paris. In London "everything was so much cleaner and quieter and drearier" than the noise and filth of Paris. Orwell also noted that English crowds were "more alike, without that fierce individuality and malice of the French."[34] "Drearier" and "malice of the French" perhaps explains why the London half lacks the arresting scenes of the Paris section.

A clearer explanation for the weakness of the London section of the book is simple. There is no one in Part II to match Boris and his unforgettable personality. Fortunately, there also is no tale comparable to Charlie's sexual adventures.

The closest creation to the lifelike Boris in the London half of the book is Bozo, the crippled pavement artist. Bozo had been a successful painter but had fallen from a roof and crushed his foot. That forced him into a life of poverty where he made his living drawing works of art on the pavement. Orwell noted that Bozo was what was called a "serious screever," that is, a pavement artist who used real painter's colors and drew political cartoons of famous people such as Winston Churchill. Orwell admired Bozo because he had educated himself – he was especially knowledgeable about astronomy. He also was fiercely proud. What impressed Orwell was Bozo's belief that no matter how poor he was, he was a free man in his mind.

The most memorable section of the London half of the book deals with how the tramps are treated by various charitable organizations. This gave Orwell an opportunity to incorporate material he had accumulated in researching "The Spike" and "Clink."

He makes it clear that tramps are never grateful for charity, especially if there are strings attached as with some of the religious establishments. Although the Salvation Army shelters are clean, he noted, they are gloomier, with an atmosphere of hopelessness, than the cheap lodging houses in London. As he observes, a man receiving charity almost always hates his benefactor.

Orwell offered no solutions for the problems of poverty that he encountered in Paris and London. His thinking hadn't yet reached that stage. The best he could offer were some generalities. Having been poor for a time, Orwell writes that he will never think that the poor are all scoundrels and villains, "nor be surprised if men out of work lack energy, . . . nor [will he] subscribe to the Salvation Army, . . . nor enjoy a meal at a smart restaurant. That is a beginning."[35]

Yes, it was a beginning. When Orwell next ventured into the land of the destitute, his thinking about the problems of poverty would crystallize.

## The Road to Wigan Pier

*Down and Out* marked the first of seven consecutive years of book-length publications. *Down and Out* was followed immediately not by further reportage, but rather by three novels, reflecting Orwell's belief that he should write fiction. At the same time, he continued reviewing for various journals although he now found *The New English Weekly*, the journal of the Social Credit movement, a more sympathetic outlet, especially after Philip Mairet took over as editor. *Adelphi* lost its appeal to Orwell as it became involved in a leftwing internal dispute. Orwell also frequently reviewed for *Time and Tide*, a politically moderate weekly that aimed at a general audience. The direct prose style of *Down and Out* and his best essays (especially "The Spike" and "A Hanging") could also be found in these reviews. He still intended to write further works of fiction, though his friend Sir Richard Rees believed that Orwell had reached a dead end with his traditional novels by the mid-1930s.

Orwell was diverted from his fiction by an idea that Gollancz hatched to capitalize on the talents that Orwell had first shown in his withering portrait of life among the downtrodden.

Although the Depression in England had moderated somewhat by the mid-1930s, some areas in the north of England and Scotland showed no signs of recovery, with the unemployment rate remaining at 25 and 30 percent. It was Gollancz's idea to commission a personalized study of an area desperately hard hit by the Depression. He believed that Orwell was the right man to do it. Orwell jumped at the chance to carry out an investigation of how the poor and unemployed dealt with the Depression. Gollancz also offered Orwell an advance of £50, a decent sum in those days.

In January 1936 Orwell took off for the north of England to begin his investigation. He would spend two months there, observing conditions, gathering information, interviewing those out of work, all the while taking voluminous notes and maintaining a diary. He told Rees that after a month he had no clear idea of how to use the material he had gathered. At one point he even thought of taking his notes and statistics and producing a book of essays about what unemployment does to the working classes. Instead he eventually produced a unique study of how the working classes deal with unemployment. In a posthumous review of the first American edition of *The Road to Wigan Pier* in 1958, critic (and no mean judge of good journalism) Dwight Macdonald described Orwell's documentary writing as "the best sociological reporting I know."

*The Road to Wigan Pier* proved to be something completely different from what Orwell had first conceived or what Gollancz expected. Like *Down and Out*, it was a work of investigation and a personal journey. But this time Orwell finally found both himself and the ultimate direction that his writing would take. He discovered his unique voice which had first surfaced in "A Hanging" and in parts of *Down and Out*. This period would also see the appearance of "Shooting an Elephant," where Orwell's mature style is clearly present.

Like *Down and Out*, *The Road to Wigan Pier* was divided into two parts. The first half is a highly personal account of the dire economic conditions prevailing in the north of England. Parts of it are a brilliant portrait of the damage that poverty inflicts. Orwell begins Part I with an unforgettable picture of a boarding house run by a disgusting family, the Brookers. This section was designed to draw the reader into the world of people on the margin of society. It contains some of Orwell's most vivid prose portraits.

Orwell describes his living quarters in the sharp detail for which he would become famous. The glass chandelier in his bedroom had "dust so thick that it was like fur."[36] The bedroom that he shared with other boarders stunk like a "ferret's cage." But his portrait of Mr. Brooker exemplified Orwell's new heights of descriptive power. "Mr. Brooker was a dark, small-boned, sour, Irish-looking man, and astonishingly dirty. I don't think I ever saw his hands clean … If he gave you a slice of bread-and-butter there was always a black thumb-print on it."[37] "Astonishing" is a perfect Orwell touch, investing filth with a sense of wonder and elevating it to a new level.

Brooker, Orwell wrote, always moved "with the incredible slowness from one hated job to another. Often the beds were still unmade at six in the evening, and at any hour of the day you were liable to meet Mr. Brooker … carrying a full chamber-pot which he gripped with his thumb well over the rim … He was one of those people who can chew their grievances like a cud." Orwell left the Brookers on the morning "when there was a full chamber-pot under the breakfast table."[38]

According to his diary, on the way north by train he saw a sight out the window that he felt compelled to write about. Even though he was at a great distance, the sight haunted him. The diary entry and the way that Orwell described the scene in *Road to Wigan Pier* are almost identical. It is an image of poverty that is truly unforgettable. A woman at the back of one of the slum houses was "poking a stick up the leaden waste-pipe . . . which was blocked . . . She knew well enough what was happening to her – understood as well as I did how dreadful a destiny it was to be kneeling there in the bitter cold, on the slimy stones of a slum backyard, poking a stick up a foul drain-pipe."[39] This is the image of poverty that Orwell wanted to convey to his middle-class audience.

The plight of the coal miners, once the elite of the English working class and now ravaged by chronic unemployment, also drew Orwell's attention. To understand their life, he spent much of his time with them and their families, seeing how they lived and how they coped with unemployment. One of his keenest observations was to note how painful it was for the working classes to go without work. Unlike intellectuals and the middle classes who usually had other options, employment defined the working classes, especially the miners. He even went down the mines to see the miners at work. At 6 foot 3 inches he could barely navigate the trip to the coal face and found walking with his knees bent physically painful after a short time. He also seriously banged his head on the shaft's ceiling.

Orwell's description of his trip to the coal face is one of the showpieces of the first part of *The Road to Wigan Pier*. He wanted to give the reader a true sense of what it was like to be a miner. He notes the immense distance the miners had to travel just to get to their work station – a mile underground on foot wasn't uncommon and in some older mines the distance could be long as five miles.

Orwell almost hero-worshipped the miners themselves who he described as resembling "iron statues" covered by "the smooth coat of coal dust which cling to them from head to foot. It is only when you see miners down a mine and naked that you realize what splendid men they are. Most of them are small . . . but nearly all of them have the most noble bodies; wide shoulders tapering to slender supple waists, and small pronounced buttocks and sinewy thighs, with not an ounce of wasted flesh anywhere."[40]

Part I of *The Road to Wigan Pier* idealizes the working classes from the viewpoint of a middle-class outsider trying to understand them. Orwell is dealing with the working poor, not the tramps and outcasts of *Down and Out*. He does not romanticize the working poor but over time develops a genuine affection for them and for the lives they follow, lives richer and more fulfilling, he believes, than those of more comfortable members of English society.

The second half of *Road to Wigan Pier* is a voyage of understanding comparable to *Down and Out*, but here Orwell is groping toward his own eccentric view of socialism. Until early 1936, Orwell's political views were radical but still largely unfocused. His trip to the north changed that. He had known socialists and had possessed some understanding of Marxist philosophy from his contacts with the *Adelphi* circle. But his investigation of the causes of poverty in the north of England forced him to think seriously whether socialism was the solution for England's economic problems.

In the second section of *The Road to Wigan Pier* Orwell deals with the paradox of socialism failing to take hold in England in the midst of the terrible economic conditions of the Depression. He begins by recounting his own political evolution. Orwell stresses the role that snobbery and class played in English life, particularly the conviction of many middle-class people that "the working classes smell." Orwell's enemies would take this comment out of context and use it against him for years. He would be charged again and again with believing that the working classes smell. No matter how many times he pointed out the context of the remark, it would be revived to use against him.

Orwell also analyzes the reasons for socialism's failure to win over the working class, blaming the faddism and eccentricity of the leftwing intellectuals and middle-class snobs.

Orwell's critique of socialism, and in particular socialists, led in the next dozen years to Orwell being increasingly viewed with suspicion by the (generally pro-communist) left in England. Part II also was something Gollancz hadn't counted on – an indictment not just of the failures of capitalism but also of the flaws in socialist thinking. Orwell's arguments about how socialism, and especially socialists, was out of touch with reality can be found in some of the most memorable passages in *The Road to Wigan Pier*. Socialism and its proponents are elitists, he wrote, smitten by industrialism and the idea of control over people's lives, not committed to justice and helping the poor. It was precisely these contentions that made Orwell controversial, indeed infamous on the British left. He was harshly critical of what Dwight Macdonald would later call "socialist romanticism about industrial progress" – or what we today would term "radical chic." Orwell believed that the leftwing intellectuals were in love with a mechanized world dependent "on the machine as the civilizations of antiquity depended on the slave."[41] At a time when the left in England, and in the West in general, was worshipping the Soviet industrial miracle, this skepticism toward industrialism and progress rendered Orwell an outcast on the left.

Despite his disgust with the blind pro-communist sympathies of many of his fellow leftists, Orwell believed that socialism constituted the only real bulwark against the greatest threat facing society, fascism. *The Road to Wigan Pier* is Orwell's first work that addresses the menace of fascism.

What worried him was the fact that socialism was perceived by many as a strange, even bizarre concept. Whenever socialists gathered, he argued, the "prevalence of cranks" undermined the movement's appeal. In one of his most frequently quoted passages, Orwell describes how socialists appear to be normal people. "One sometimes gets the impression that the mere words 'Socialism' and 'Communism' draw towards them with magnetic force every fruit-juice drinker, nudist, sandal-wearer, sex-maniac, Quaker, 'Nature Cure' quack, pacifist, and feminist in England."[42]

Unless socialism loses its "crank" image, Orwell argues, it will never win over either the working classes or the middle classes necessary for it to come to power. He believed that it was necessary for him to point out socialism's flaws, serving as a kind of Devil's advocate for the cause. Socialism should emphasize "justice and common decency" and avoid its crankier ideas.

When Gollancz received the manuscript of *The Road to Wigan Pier*, he was thrilled with Part I. It was everything he wanted, and especially suitable for his new project, the Left Book Club. Gollancz lobbied Orwell to publish Part I as the Left Book Club choice of the month but Orwell demurred. He said it would have to be all of *The Road to Wigan Pier* or nothing. Gollancz decided to go ahead and publish the entire book as part of the Left Book Club series which would guarantee large sales, as the Club membership was growing weekly. To get around his problem with Part II and to soothe the feelings of his largely leftwing audience, Gollancz added a thirteen-page foreword where he took issue with some of Orwell's ideas.

When Orwell's book came out, various writers on the left criticized it for failing to let the facts speak for themselves. They charged that he was at fault for putting too much of himself in the narrative and that the heavily autobiographical Part 2 was a travesty that tried to shift the reader's attention from the really important social problems to the insignificant life of "a disillusioned little middle-class boy . . . and late imperial policeman" as Harry Pollitt called him in the *Daily Worker*.[43]

*The Road to Wigan Pier* was published in March 1937 and eventually sold more than 40,000 copies. Including his advance of £50, Orwell made more money from *The Road to Wigan Pier* (£549) than from all his past writings. It made Orwell well known in political and literary circles in England. It also made him a hated enemy to many on the left, especially communists in England, a hatred that would deepen with his writings about the Spanish Civil War.

## Homage to Catalonia

Orwell's last and greatest piece of documentary prose emerged from his growing concern about the rise of fascism. As early as 1934 he had begun thinking seriously about the implications of fascism for England, its connection to the decline of capitalism, and its relationship to socialism. Orwell became one of the few observers to see that fascism was something more than an outgrowth of capitalism in decline – indeed that it was in some way a perversion of socialism. Even as he was writing *The Road to Wigan Pier* in 1936, he closely followed events in Spain where a civil war had erupted in July. Early in the fall of 1936 he decided to go to Spain, both to report on the war and to take part in the fighting.

Initially Orwell wanted to join the communist-controlled International Brigades which had a reputation of being the most aggressive branch of the anti-fascist movement. Because of his criticisms of communism in *The Road to Wigan Pier* and elsewhere, Orwell found it impossible to get letters of introduction from Harry Pollitt, the head of the Communist Party in England. Pollitt, who had negatively reviewed *The Road to Wigan Pier*, regarded Orwell as "politically unreliable," marking the start of a campaign to belittle him that would grow with intensity after Orwell began writing about his Spanish experiences.

Orwell received a letter of introduction from Fenner Brockway, one of the leading figures in the Independent Labour Party (ILP) to John McNair, the party's representative in Barcelona. The ILP was connected to the more radical anti-communist leftwing groups in Spain. Moreover, the ILP's independent political stance suited Orwell's own unpredictable leftwing views at the time.

Orwell left England in December 1936, arriving in Barcelona in early January. There he joined the Partido Obrero de Unificacion Marxista or POUM, a radical leftwing movement with a mix of anarchist and Trotskyist leanings. The POUM was committed to the idea that the war and the revolution were one, a concept derived from Trotsky's slogan, "the war and the revolution are inseparable." This contrasted with the position of the communist-dominated Republican movement for "war now, revolution later." At this time Orwell did not clearly understand all the myriad distinctions among the various anti-fascist groups in Spain. He simply wanted to get to the front and fight fascism.

Orwell's six months in Spain would complete his political education. His Spanish experiences would also give birth to the book that finally defined his political views, *Homage to Catalonia*. The title itself is revealing in many

ways of Orwell's scrupulous regard for the truth. He was paying homage to
the men with whom he fought against fascism. Since his experiences were
limited to Catalonia, however, he didn't pretend he knew what was happening in all parts of Spain. Thus his "homage" was exclusively to Catalonia, not
to Spain.

Orwell's six months in Spain not only completed his political education but
also gave him first-hand experience of war. In a strange yet typical way, he
enjoyed his time at the front despite all its deprivations. He particularly
enjoyed the comradeship with his men. When he first arrived in Barcelona at
the Lenin Barracks, one of the soldiers greeted him and shook his hand, calling
him "Comrade," which touched Orwell's sense of egalitarianism. He also was
deeply moved by his initial impression of Barcelona, then in the midst of
enormous enthusiasm for the fight against fascism. "Waiters treated you as an
equal," he wrote of his initial breath of the air of revolution. "Servile speech had
disappeared . . . people believed that all men are equal and acted on their belief.
The result was a feeling of liberation and hope that is difficult to conceive . . ."
Orwell found this "queer and moving . . . I recognized it immediately as a state
of affairs worth fighting for."[44]

Orwell would never forget those first days in Spain. The anger he felt at the
betrayal of the revolution would run through all his writings thereafter, first in
his Catalonian memoir and then in essays and journalism expressing his
contempt for those leftists who had betrayed the cause.

Orwell spent 115 days at the front and came under fire a number of times.
Most of the time life in the front lines was boring. He read constantly, tried
to make notes of his experiences and in general absorb the world of the
infantryman. Because of his experience in the Imperial Police he was made
a corporal or *cabo* and put in charge of a twelve-man squad. He captured the
atmosphere of life at the front perfectly, in which boredom alternated with
moments of sheer panic when fighting broke out. On one occasion he was
on sniper duty and saw a fascist soldier dropping his pants to defecate. He
couldn't bring himself to shoot the enemy because such a man was "not a
fascist but a fellow human being."[45]

According to one of his comrades, Orwell was "absolutely fearless." In an
attack on the fascist frontlines near Huesca on the Aragon front, Orwell took
part in one of the few major military actions of his service. It was the only time
he became engaged in hand-to-hand fighting. He was responsible for knocking
out a machine gun nest. He threw a grenade that in his words "by a stroke of
luck" landed where the machine gun was placed. "Instantly there was a
diabolical outcry of screams and groans. Poor wretch! Poor wretch! I felt a
vague sorrow."[46]

While he was at the front Orwell had little idea of what was happening to the revolution in Spain until he returned to Barcelona in May 1937. He discovered that the communists who controlled the Spanish government had decided to purge the Republican forces of its anarchist and Trotskyist elements, including the POUM. These orders had come from the Soviet Union. Orwell and his wife Eileen, who had traveled to Spain to be close to him, were caught in the fighting. Orwell was outraged that the revolutionary spirit of Barcelona had dissolved and that his friends in the POUM were now being labeled fascist sympathizers and traitors. Posters appeared throughout Barcelona that showed POUM soldiers unmasked and their faces bearing a swastika. The communists accused POUM of being part of Franco's Fifth Column, a charge that Orwell found unforgiveable. More than 400 people, mostly from the POUM and its allies, were killed in the May fighting. Orwell never forgot the lies and distortion he witnessed during these days. From this point Orwell's suspicion of communism (or what he preferred to call "Stalinism") deepened into a hatred that endured for of the rest of his life. Exposing the lies of the communists became a theme he would pursue in some of his best writings.

After the street fighting in Barcelona in May, Orwell returned to the Aragon front. Ten days later, he was shot in the throat. He came within millimeters of losing his life. After his recovery, he discovered that he was on the communist purge list and fled Spain with his wife in June 1937. Orwell never knew just how close he had come to death. After the collapse of communism in Russia, the Soviet archives revealed that Orwell had been labeled a Trotskyite in contact with dissident elements in Moscow. He was marked for arrest and execution if captured. This was no mere threat; hundreds, if not thousands, of anti-communists were shot and killed on Russian orders.

On his return to England he immediately began recording his Spanish experiences, determined to tell the truth of what he saw. He offered his reportage to the *New Statesman*, the leading leftwing magazine in England, only to have it rejected. The editor, Kingsley Martin, said he couldn't publish Orwell's material because it contradicted the magazine's political stance of supporting the communist-dominated government in Spain. As a sop he offered Orwell a book on the Spanish situation to review (Franz Borkenau, *The Spanish Cockpit*) and then rejected that also because of Orwell's interpretation of the civil war. Orwell was outraged not just by the refusal to publish an unpopular interpretation of events, but also by this blatant disregard for historical truth. He rejected Martin's offer to pay him for the unpublished reviews. The Spanish Civil War not only turned Orwell into an impassioned anti-communist, but it also prompted his growing awareness that the very concept of historical truth was disappearing amidst the clash of competing ideologies. In a later essay, "Looking Back on the Spanish War" written during World War II, Orwell reverted to this theme. In Spain, Orwell wrote:

> I saw newspaper reports which did not bear any relation to the facts, not even the relationship which is implied in an ordinary lie. I saw great battles reported where there had been no fighting, and complete silence where hundreds of men had been killed. I saw troops who had fought bravely denounced as cowards and traitors, and others who had never seen a shot fired hailed as heroes of imaginary victories; and I saw newspapers in London retailing these lies and eager intellectuals building emotional superstructures over events that had never happened. I saw, in fact, history being written not in terms of what happened but of what ought to have happened according to various "party lines."[47]

The themes that would dominate *Animal Farm* and *Nineteen Eighty-Four* now began to take shape in his mind.

Orwell began his Spanish memoir in July, almost immediately on his return to England. It was written in a blaze of anger and completed by the fall of 1937. He offered *Homage to Catalonia* to his publisher Victor Gollancz, who rejected it out of hand also for ideological reasons. That didn't surprise Orwell, who called Gollancz "part of the Communist racket." What made Orwell anathema in communist circles was the conclusion he drew from his time in Spain that "official Communism must be regarded. . .as an anti-revolutionary force." He also pointed out that communists in Spain wanted not just "to postpone the Spanish revolution but to make sure it never happened."[48] These views outraged English leftwingers.

Orwell struggled to find a publisher. Then Frederic Warburg of Secker & Warburg, a small, newly founded press with good contacts in radical leftwing circles, agreed to bring it out.

*Homage to Catalonia* appeared in April 1938. Because of the Popular Front atmosphere of the day it was barely reviewed. *Homage to Catalonia* sold less than a thousand copies during Orwell's lifetime. Despite this fact he regarded it – along with *Animal Farm* – as one of the books he was most proud to have written.

Although Orwell began writing a new novel almost as soon as *Homage to Catalonia* was published, for the next six years his interest shifted away from fiction to political journalism or reportage. After the 1939 publication of his novel, *Coming Up for Air*, he never wrote another traditional novel. His deepened interest in political writing carried over to his reviewing. After 1938 he tended to review works of fact rather than novels. As Orwell noted in his essay "Why I Write," "Every line of serious work that I have written since

1936 has been written, directly or indirectly, against totalitarianism and for Socialism, as I understand it. It seems to me nonsense, in a period like our own, to think that one can avoid writing of such subjects."[49]

## Orwell the essayist

George Orwell penned a considerable body of writing: four traditional novels, two satirical masterpieces as well as two works of brilliant sociological-political reportage. But a genre that he excelled in, the essay, has been largely neglected by the public, even though his short non-fictional prose is highly regarded by specialists in Orwell's writings.

Orwell wrote constantly during the first decade of his literary life. Despite serious health problems and the need to take menial jobs, he barely eked out a living through his writing. According to an analysis by Peter Davison, Orwell's income from his reviews and essays for those years was £164, or an average of just under £18 a year.

Orwell also dabbled in poetry during the 1930s, although most of his poems are not highly regarded today. There is evidence that Orwell enjoyed writing poetry and one or two pieces show his skill at using the clear, vivid English he later became famous for. "The Crystal Spirit" shows Orwell at his best, with its last stanza about his Italian comrade in Spain.

> But the thing that I saw in your face
> No power can disinherit:
> No bomb that ever burst
> Shatters the crystal spirit.[50]

Orwell also did considerable reviewing during the 1930s, initially for *Adelphi*, which served as his real training ground, and then from 1935 on for the *New English Weekly*, whose editors allowed him freedom to review what he liked. Late in the decade his reviews and articles began to appear in more popular and influential journals, such as *The Listener*, *Fortnightly Review*, *Time and Tide*, and the *New Statesman*. By the outbreak of World War II Orwell had become a superb reviewer, getting to the heart of the book in question quickly and then using the review to advance some of his own ideas and insights.

Classic examples of Orwell's skill can be found in two of his reviews in 1940. In an appreciation of Malcolm Muggeridge's popular history, *The Thirties*, entitled appropriately enough, "The Limits of Pessimism," Orwell praised Muggeridge's portrait as "nearer to essential truth" of that decade than any other book written. Then after a survey of the highlights of that "low, dishonest decade," Orwell ends his review with a long paragraph that reveals where his thinking was heading as the war broke out. Orwell had briefly flirted with pacifism after he returned from Spain but that phase passed as war approached.

What Muggeridge reflects, Orwell wrote, is "the emotions of the middle-class man, brought up in the military tradition, who finds in the moment of crisis that he is a patriot after all." It is typical of leftwing intellectuals to snigger at patriotism, Orwell argued, "but a time comes when the sand of the desert is sodden red and what have I done for thee, England my England."[51] Orwell had captured the mood of the nation as the Phony War came to an end.

Orwell also reviewed Hitler's *Mein Kampf* at approximately the same time, early in 1940. He begins with a remark that few English would have made at that time: "I have never been able to dislike Hitler." Orwell even goes so far as to compare the pained look on Hitler's face in certain photographs to that of the crucified Christ. But he focuses on an aspect of Hitler's appeal that most English intellectuals missed – his demand that the German people turn their backs on materialism and the falsity of the hedonist life. Hitler offers the German people "struggle, danger and death," Orwell wrote, for which they throw themselves at his feet. That appeal is beyond the imagination of any English intellectual Orwell argued, but it shows Hitler's superior understanding of human nature.[52] This was Orwell's way of showing how shallow the thinking of the left was at this time, talking about materialism when England's fate was at stake. His kind of leftwing patriotism distinguished him from many of his fellow leftists.

Between 1931 and England's moment of crisis in the dangerous summer of 1940 Orwell found time amidst his other writings, his travels through the north of England, and his six months in Spain to produce a half-dozen major essays. Included in that group were two unforgettable masterpieces, "A Hanging" and "Shooting an Elephant," along with a handful of short pieces that show Orwell groping toward a mastery of this seemingly simple, yet difficult, literary form.

Orwell's essays, like his novels in the 1930s, drew directly on his experiences. One thing is clear – he was not interested in the belles-lettres concept of the essay. There was a powerful, if sometimes vague, political motivation behind almost everything he wrote in the 1930s, even in his seemingly non-political writings. As he slowly defined his political views, certain themes emerged: hatred of imperialism, an embrace of a singular form of socialism, and a fear of fascism. These themes dominate his best essays written in the years leading up to World War II.

Orwell did not concentrate on the traditional essay form at first. He was too busy with his attempts at fiction to devote much time to the essay format. Two essays, "Hop-Picking" and "The Spike," were among his first serious publications in 1931. He later recycled material from them into his novels.

Orwell wrote a half-dozen important essays by the outbreak of the war. All of them are derived from his experiences. "Bookshop Memories," written in 1936, reflects a degree of disgust on Orwell's part for what he had to do to pursue his career as a writer. It also reveals Orwell's skill at extracting significant insights from otherwise trivial matters.

Orwell's fifteen months working at Booklover's Corner in Hampstead, London, provided him with useful material for his novel *Keep the Aspidistra Flying*. But he came to resent the time he had wasted and poured out his anger in "Bookshop Memories." It was a typical example of the kind of essay Orwell was experimenting with and one that revealed his gift for caricature and exaggeration as well as some half-serious, half-humorous perceptions. Working in a bookstore, he discovered, instead of being "a kind of paradise," turned into a nuisance. Instead of dealing with booklovers, Orwell was confronted by "vague-minded women looking for birthday presents" or "oriental students haggling over cheap textbooks." Bookstores attracted "certifiable lunatics," Orwell claimed, because they can loiter as long as they want without spending any money. Being forced to deal with cranks that inhabit book stores, with having to run a lending library of books he considered worthless, and with having to sell horoscopes and Christmas cards showing, for example, the "Infant Jesus with rabbits," was too much for Orwell.

Orwell wrote that his bookshop experience ruined his "love for books." At one time, I "really did love books – loved the sight and smell and feel of them . . . But as soon as I went to work in the bookshop I stopped buying books." The very sight of books in a mass he suddenly found "slightly sickening" while their "sweet smell of decaying paper" was now "closely associated in my mind with paranoiac customers and dead bluebottles."[53]

"Bookshop Memories" revealed Orwell's talent for creating a mood. The emphasis on odors and smells, the proliferation of the odd and eccentric characters were typical of Orwell's developing approach to the essay. While "Bookshop Memories" does not deal with the world of politics, Orwell managed to find a political angle – he stresses the way the book companies force magazines to provide decent, if meaningless, reviews – a kind of "you scratch my back and I will scratch yours."

The essay is also an example of how Orwell would take an everyday experience and draw general lessons from it. His literary skills were growing.

## "A Hanging" and "Shooting an Elephant"

The two essays that were derived from Orwell's time in Burma, "A Hanging" and "Shooting an Elephant," were unique. The subject matter was unusual – a brutal execution and the shooting of a rogue elephant – and not typical of the type of essay published at that time. Questions have been raised whether the two essays are based on events in Orwell's life or whether they were examples of his developing imaginative powers. The majority opinion is that they were real incidents reshaped by Orwell, a skill that he also practiced in his semi-autobiographical novels.

During his time in Burma there were more than 150 executions a year. Witnessing one would have been a distinct possibility for him. Michael Shelden believes that the very detail of "A Hanging" argues for its authenticity. Gordon Bowker, in his biography of Orwell, sees a literary connection between "A Hanging" and a short story, "The Vice Consul," by Somerset Maugham, an author Orwell deeply admired.[54]

"A Hanging" appeared under Orwell's real name in August 1931 in *Adelphi* and is the earliest example of his emerging potential as a writer. The essay powerfully retells the last few minutes in the life of a "Hindu, a puny wisp of a man" as Orwell describes him. Orwell portrayed the hanging in a way that immediately seizes the reader's attention with a dramatic opening. "I saw a man hanged once; it seemed to me worse than a thousand deaths."[55]

What gives the essay force is the detail Orwell weaves through it. The condemned man loses control of his bladder when he hears the death sentence confirmed. As he is being marched to his death, Orwell focuses intensely on the scene. His description of the prisoner evokes his humanity. He walked with the "bobbling gate of the Indian who never straightens his knees. At each step his muscles slid neatly into place, the lock of hair on his scalp danced up and down, his feet printed themselves on the wet gravel. And once, in spite of the men who gripped him by each shoulder, he stepped slightly aside to avoid a puddle."[56]

At this point Orwell interjects himself into the essay. "It is curious," he wrote, "but till that moment I had never realized what it means to destroy a healthy, conscious man. When I saw the prisoner step aside to avoid the puddle, I saw the mystery, the unspeakable wrongness of cutting a life short when it is in full tide."[57]

Orwell further humanizes the incident when a dog suddenly appears. Orwell uses its appearance to contrast its mundane actions with the ghastly fate that awaits the condemned prisoner. Before anyone could stop it the dog "made a mad dash for the prisoner, and jumping up tried to lick his face." Left implied by Orwell was that this action by the dog was the only kindly or comforting action the condemned man received.[58]

"A Hanging" enables Orwell to show a moment of greater truth, an epiphany, when he recognizes the humanity of the man about to be hanged.

"A Hanging" is an immensely powerful and mature piece of writing and reveals how far Orwell had come by 1931 in his determination to be a writer. It also shows how he could take a seemingly prosaic action and find deeper meaning. "Shooting an Elephant" would remove any doubts about his skill and demonstrate a mastery of the essay form.

"Shooting an Elephant" was written in 1936 in answer to John Lehmann's request for Orwell to contribute something for the recently established Penguin journal, *New Writing*. Lehmann catered to the writers of the Auden generation yet knew Orwell's work and took a chance that he might have something worthwhile. He was correct.

Orwell said that he wrote the piece in two weeks and finished it three days before he was married to Eileen O'Shaughnessy in June 1936. It appeared the following November as Lehmann knew he had something special.

Besides *Animal Farm* and *Nineteen Eighty-Four*, "Shooting an Elephant" is Orwell's best-known work. For someone wishing to dip into Orwell's writing, it is the best introduction. It is brief – only seven pages – and was anthologized for years in high school and university English texts, quickly becoming part of the canon throughout the English-speaking world. It has been read and enjoyed by four generations of students. Written at a time when Orwell was still convinced that his future lay in fiction, the essay shows better than anything else that Orwell had found his voice.

"Shooting an Elephant" has generated controversy as to whether the event really happened. Attempts have been made to discover whether any elephants were shot while Orwell served in Burma. But the historical accuracy of the essay is beside the point. What renders it outstanding is the sharpness of the detail and even the poignancy of the telling. It is also a superb example of the narrative ability Orwell was developing of standing outside an event that he was a part of.

The essay begins with another of Orwell's classic opening lines. "In Moulmein, in Lower Burma, I was hated by large numbers of people – the only time in my life I have been important enough for this to happen to me."[59] It is perhaps worth noting that Moulmein is mentioned in Kipling's famous poem "On the Road to Mandalay," a poem that Orwell would cite as conveying powerful memories of Burma for him. He had written a brief appreciation of Kipling for *New English Weekly* in January, just a few months before writing "Shooting an Elephant" and quoted from "On the Road to Mandalay" as an example of Kipling's ability to create an evocative image.

The plot of "Shooting An Elephant" is a simple one. A working elephant had turned rogue and is ravaging the local bazaar. It destroys the villagers' huts, kills a cow, and eats food from the village stalls. Orwell, as the policeman in charge, is called on to take charge of the elephant.

The incident was a small one, not uncommon in a country where elephants did much of the heavy work. From it, however, Orwell marshals a powerful attack on the idea of Empire, but he does so in a highly personal, and clever, way.

When he comes across the elephant it has quietened down and is no longer a threat to anyone. But it had killed "an Indian, a black Dravidian coolie." Orwell's description of the dead "coolie" is designed to emphasize his humanity. "This was the rainy season and the ground was soft and his face had scored a trench a foot deep . . . He was lying on his belly with arms crucified and head sharply twisted to one side."[60] The image is an interesting one, evoking the crucified Christ on the cross. The death of the "coolie" means that Orwell would have to kill the elephant not because he has to – the elephant is now quiet – but because the people demand it of him.

The issue was pointless but he knew what he had to do – "a sahib has got to act like a sahib." Pressured by the mob, who Orwell paints in all its unpleasant features, he kills the elephant. The description of the elephant's death is an example of the power of Orwell's prose. As he does with the dead "coolie," Orwell humanizes and evokes pity for the elephant. After Orwell shoots, "a mysterious, terrible change had come over the elephant. He neither stirred nor fell, but every line of his body had altered. He looked suddenly stricken, shrunken, immensely old . . ." To put the elephant out of his misery Orwell had to pour shot after shot down the "caverns of pale pink throat" to the cheers of the mob. Eventually the elephant dies and within minutes the villagers had stripped its body to the bone. Peter Davison has compared the slow death of the elephant (and Orwell's empathy for it) "to the last throes of the Raj itself."[61]

Orwell hadn't wanted to kill the elephant but the crowd forced his hand. The lesson Orwell drew from that fact shaped his distinctive analysis of the evils of imperialism. Orwell noted that the life of a white man in the East was "one long struggle not to be laughed at." "When the white man turns tyrant," he argued, "it is his own freedom that he destroys."[62]

## Inside the Whale

Orwell did not devote much time to essay writing after the publication of "Shooting an Elephant" in 1936. He was busy with his two documentary studies on Wigan and the war in Spain. But in 1939, after finishing *Coming*

*Up for Air*, he began writing a series of sketches on topics targeted at a middle-class audience. He told his friend Geoffrey Gorer that the essays would be in the nature of "semi-sociological literary criticism."

Orwell was attempting something different, writing about literature in a unique way. The three essays he was working on dealt with Charles Dickens, boys' magazines and the writer Henry Miller. Although these essays dealt with literary themes, there was a decided political undercurrent in them. Dickens and Miller had no time for politics or political nostrums, while the boys' magazines were also apolitical and frozen in a time warp, before World War I. But to the politically engaged Orwell that didn't matter. All three essays touched on deep elements of the human spirit and said important things about the political culture of the day.

Eventually the three essays were gathered together and published under the title of the Miller essay, *Inside the Whale*. With this volume Orwell was doing something unusual – examining three different types of literature from a unique standpoint, in the process inaugurating a new field of popular culture studies. As Peter Davison notes, with these essays Orwell effectively was "broadening and redefining concepts of culture."[63]

*Inside the Whale* was published in March 1940 at the height of the Phony War and proved groundbreaking. "Charles Dickens" took a fresh look at a novelist who Orwell deeply admired and whom he noted "is one of those writers well worth stealing." Even today, more than seventy years after it appeared, it is still highly regarded among Dickens scholars. Orwell's contribution to Dickens scholarship was recognized at the time. He was asked to lecture to the influential Dickens Fellowship. The invitation took on special meaning as one of Orwell's idols, Compton Mackenzie, agreed to chair the session.

Orwell saw Dickens as a moralist with a profound sympathy for the oppressed victims of the emerging British capitalist system. Dickens was a nineteenth-century radical who represented the decency of the engaged writer, in Orwell's eyes. But he had no political solutions to England's problems because he was disgusted by politics and politicians – despite the fact that Dickens wrote at a time when the Victorian giants, William Gladstone and Benjamin Disraeli, were at the peak of their careers. Despite Dickens's limitations, Orwell admired him and believed that by calling for people to act decently toward each other, some of the evils of society would be mitigated.

Orwell also was impressed by how the English public still cherished Dickens with his uncomplicated decency and his appeals to simple justice. Orwell contrasted their reaction to the way the English intelligentsia in his lifetime embraced one form of totalitarianism or another.

There are aspects of the Dickens essay where one clearly sees his influence on Orwell. Indeed at times it almost seems that Orwell is writing not about Dickens but about himself. When he visualizes Dickens, Orwell sees "the face of a man who is always fighting against something but who fights in the open and is not frightened, the face of a man who generously angry . . . a type hated with equal hatred by all the smelly little orthodoxies which are now contending for our souls . . ."[64]

The second essay in *Inside the Whale* was one that was close to Orwell's heart. "Boys' Weeklies" dealt with the popular comic magazines, particularly *Magnet* and *Gem*, which were popular in the years before World War I. Orwell, who romanticized those years, never lost his affection for the magazines. Writing about them provided Orwell with an excuse to relive a part of the past that he remembered fondly – an Edwardian world frozen in time. He defended the magazines' worldview, which was deeply patriotic and found all foreigners amusing, England's leaders brave, and the working class funny. The political ideology of the magazines preached conservative values, he noted, but the magazines had no connection to the totalitarianisms of the present day. Orwell lamented that there were no leftwing comic strips to teach the values of socialism, but believed that it would be impossible to create one.

What makes "Boys' Weeklies" so significant is that the essay is the forerunner of the discipline of cultural studies. No one before Orwell had thought it important enough to produce serious studies of what was essentially ephemeral popular material. In that sense he was a founder of a whole new field of study.

Henry Miller was an American author whose books *Tropic of Cancer* and *Black Monday* were considered pornographic at the time. Like Dickens, Miller had no interest in political matters. Despite that fact, Orwell admired Miller, who he argued understood the essence of life and wrote about real people. Orwell called him, with considerable exaggeration, "the only imaginative prose writer . . . who has appeared among the English-speaking races for some years."[65] Where that puts James Joyce and Ernest Hemingway, among others, is difficult to say.

What makes the Miller essay significant is the way Orwell analyzes the literary developments of the post-World War I era. After first discussing the Modernists of the 1920s – D. H. Lawrence, Yeats, James Joyce – whom Orwell admired but whom he labeled escapists politically, he describes Miller as someone, despite his fascination with the underside of society, who is writing about the real world. He further compares Miller favorably to what Orwell called the Auden–C. Day Lewis–Spender generation of politically engaged writers in the 1930s. Miller, Orwell argues, understood the working classes, their needs and their desires, while the Auden–Spender group are dilettantes attracted to the politically fashionable Marxism of the day. Worse, they are, in Orwell's view, insincere poseurs playing at radical politics. These writers also are products of the public school and London literary circuit – "moneyed-beasts" Orwell calls them – a social set with which he was never comfortable.

Orwell was particularly cruel about Auden, whom he had described in *The Road to Wigan Pier* as a "gutless Kipling." Citing a line from one of Auden's poems about Spain in which he compares the boring meeting to the necessary murder, Orwell wrote in the Miller essay that "I would not speak so lightly of murder." "To me, murder is something to be avoided." What Auden is doing, according to Orwell, is akin to "playing with fire by people who don't even know the fire is hot." "Mr. Auden's brand of amoralism," according to Orwell "is only possible if you are the kind of person who is always somewhere else when the trigger is pulled."[66] Orwell seems to be saying that this kind of nonsense is something that Henry Miller would never fall victim to.

Orwell may have been angry at Auden for leaving England just as the war broke out. Evelyn Waugh also was angry and would later parody Auden and Stephen Spender as "Parsnip and Pimpernel" in his satiric portrait of the Phony War, *Put Out More Flags.* Interestingly, Orwell and Auden later became friends. Orwell found it difficult to be angry at anyone once he got to know them.

The Miller essay became a standard analysis that shaped criticism regarding the literary trends of the generation of writers after World War I.

## *Critical Essays*

After World War II broke out, Orwell's literary output was concentrated overwhelmingly on political matters. During 1940 he wrote a small but influential book, *The Lion and the Unicorn*, which dealt with the importance of the middle classes and working classes cooperating around the idea of patriotism to win the war and to bring about a genuine social revolution. He tried desperately to find significant war work but was unsuccessful for health reasons. As a consolation in June 1940 he joined the Home Guard where he was a serious and active member, reaching the rank of sergeant because of his military experience in Spain. In August 1941 he began work at the BBC producing broadcasts to India, a position he held for two years. Until he began writing *Animal Farm* late in 1943, most of Orwell's literary endeavors during the war years (other than *The Lion and the Unicorn*) were reviews and essays. The essays in the last decade of his life built on the foundation he laid in *Inside the Whale*. They were written in the highly personal documentary prose style that Orwell had mastered.

The essays he wrote in the middle years of the 1940s had two broad themes: an interest in the popular literature and popular art to see what they said about developments in English culture and, at a more significant level, by what he saw as the debasement of the language. He was fearful that this corruption of the language (not just by totalitarian regimes but also by the Western democracies) would lead eventually to the loss of the concept of objective truth. Although his essays during these years often dealt with seemingly insignificant topics (toads, how to make a cup of tea, comic postcards, an ideal pub, a defense of English cooking, murder mysteries, etc.), they contained a deeper message and pointed the way to the two seminal works of the last years of his life.

In late 1944 shortly after Orwell had finished *Animal Farm*, he decided to bring together a collection of the best essays he had written since *Inside the Whale*. Among other things they would comprise his insights on the major literary figures such as H. G. Wells, Yeats, Rudyard Kipling, and Tolstoy who had influenced him. But Orwell was not writing literary criticism as much as pioneering in a new field, cultural studies, even if he never named it as such.

Orwell thought these pieces, which he called *Critical Essays*, important enough to have them published in book form because otherwise he feared they might be forgotten. In November 1947 when Frederic Warburg decided to produce a unified edition of his writings, Orwell listed *Critical Essays* third in importance, just after *Animal Farm* and *Homage to Catalonia*.[67]

Orwell had grown confident of his ability to produce short, insightful pieces on unusual topics. The ten essays that comprised *Critical Essays* (the American edition was called *Dickens, Dali and Others*) show Orwell at his best. They included such classics as "Raffles and Miss Blandish" on the crucial difference between American and English detective stories; "Benefit of Clergy," in which Orwell indicts the sadism he finds in Salvador Dalí's art, and "Looking Back on the Spanish War," first written in 1942, a powerful indictment of the failure of the English intelligentsia to think clearly about the issues in the Spanish Civil War. The latter also dealt with Orwell's concern, first voiced in reviews and essays when he returned from Spain, that the very concept of historical objectivity was disappearing in the West. Orwell wrote that he had found the leftwing English press reporting events that had never taken place and distorting the facts of the war. The seeds of *Animal Farm* and *Nineteen Eighty-Four* can be found in Orwell's thoughts on the loss of truth about Spain.

All the essays showed Orwell's talent for finding deep meaning in otherwise trivial matters. But the overriding theme in the essays was how the debasement of the English language was corrupting the political scene.

Typical of Orwell's approach was his essay "The Art of Donald McGill." McGill produced humorous postcards of fat women and hen-pecked husbands. Orwell, an inveterate collector of such ephemera, found McGill's work crude but life-affirming. In a typical insight similar to his defense of boys' weeklies he voiced suspicion of those who denigrated such expressions of popular culture. Feminist writers have taken a dim view of Orwell's defense of McGill. Daphne Patai in her critique of Orwell's misogyny, *The Orwell Mystique*, labeled the McGill essay as "anti-woman." She argued that Orwell wasn't capable of analyzing "the ideology of gender roles depicted in McGill's postcards."[68] What she misses is the simple fact that Orwell found the post-cards funny. Shelden compares Orwell's defense of McGill's artwork to Winston Smith's attachment to the glass paperweight in *Nineteen Eighty-Four*, an example of the way insignificant things can be life-affirming.[69]

Orwell also included a defense of Rudyard Kipling in *Critical Essays*. He had first expressed admiration for Kipling in a short piece written just after the poet's death in 1936. He elaborated on that in an essay written originally for *Horizon* in 1942. Kipling meant a great deal to Orwell. He was part of that Edwardian world that he had grown up in and which Orwell had a tendency to romanticize. Orwell described Kipling as an example of a good–bad poet/writer, a concept he borrowed from G. K. Chesterton. Kipling's philosophy of life, especially his defense of the British Empire, was wrong but Orwell rejected the view then current that he was a forerunner of fascism.

Kipling, Orwell argued, would be remembered because he contributed so many favorite phrases to the English language – "East is East, and West is West," "the female of the species is more deadly than the male," "somewhere East of Suez," etc. For all his political flaws, Orwell admired Kipling because he was not a product of the public school Oxbridge–London literary circuit. Orwell also argued that Kipling had a sense of responsibility unlike his con-temporaries such as Oscar Wilde and Shaw. Wilde's "epigrams" and Shaw's "cracker-mottoes," Orwell argued, appear shallow and irritating, while Kipling's writings are still remembered.

> Orwell ... took great pleasure in portraying Kipling as a model of literary activism from whom the contemporary "pansy left" could learn some valuable lessons. In an age of mass indifference to literature, Kipling managed to appeal to the public by writing numerous poems ... in which poetic diction had been grafted onto everyday feelings. He had ennobled the outlook of the common man by transfiguring it into verse ... Kipling's generation of imperialists might have been odious but at least they were "people who did things ... they changed the face of the earth."[70]

*Critical Essays* appeared in England in February 1946, with the American edition being published three months later. Coming so soon after *Animal Farm*, *Critical Essays* reaffirmed the level of literary skill that Orwell had achieved by the mid-1940s. On both sides of the Atlantic he was hailed as a writer who was well worth reading and as a critic whose insights were original and always compelling.

In April 1946, at almost the same time as *Critical Essays* appeared, Orwell published one of his most quoted essays also in *Horizon*, "Politics and the English Language." Like "Shooting an Elephant," this essay became part of the English school canon for years. It is full of good advice, common sense and even a sense of humor. Orwell's six rules of good writing have been cited as examples of how to produce clear prose.

> 1.Never use a metaphor, simile or other figure of speech, which you are used to seeing in print. 2. Never use a long word where a short one will do. 3. If it is possible to cut a word, always cut it out. 4. Never use the passive where you can use the active. 5. Never use a foreign phrase, a scientific word or a jargon word if you can think of an everyday English equivalent. 6. Break any of these rules sooner than say anything outright barbarous.[71]

Rule number 6 is typical of Orwell as well as an effective answer to those who would find his rules pompous.

## *Animal Farm*

After publishing *Coming Up for Air* in 1939, Orwell wrote only one book-length manuscript during the next six years. *The Lion and the Unicorn*, which he published in February 1941, was the first in Secker & Warburg's Searchlight Books series. Orwell's timing for once was perfect. With the threat of a German invasion hanging over the country, *The Lion and the Unicorn* appeared during one of the most dangerous periods in British history and sold well. It also helped solidify Orwell's reputation as a writer worth reading.

For Britain to survive the war, Orwell argued, a genuine revolution was necessary. The glue that would hold the working and middle classes together to unite them behind this revolution was "the overwhelming strength of patriotism, national loyalty."[72] Orwell aimed to rescue the concept of patriotism from the disrepute it had fallen into after World War I. A patriot himself, he perceived that the innate love of country felt by the lower and middle classes could serve as the rallying point for the true revolution that Britain needed.

By the time that *The Lion and the Unicorn* appeared in early 1941, Orwell recognized that the revolutionary moment had passed. Britain was now confronted with a desperate struggle for survival. He still believed in the idea of revolution and hoped that the war would somehow radicalize the British public. At the same time, Orwell struggled without much success to find a role for himself in the conflict. His two years at the BBC broadcasting propaganda to India left him disillusioned. In his letter of resignation in November 1943, Orwell told his superiors that he was leaving because he had been wasting his time and the government's money on work that had no meaningful result.

Orwell left the BBC to become literary editor of the leftwing weekly, *Tribune*. He felt comfortable at *Tribune* because, under the guidance of the radical Labour MP Aneurin Bevan, it was solidly leftist without being Stalinist. Bevan gave Orwell a free hand and didn't interfere even when some of his opinions outraged *Tribune*'s readers. Along with his editorial duties, Orwell wrote a highly provocative, idiosyncratic column, "As I Please," in which he voiced his opinions on any political, literary, or cultural issue that interested him. However, his friends admitted, Orwell was a poor editor. Perhaps remembering his own struggles to get published, he was too kind-hearted to reject material and often gave out book reviews to desperate writers.[73]

Orwell spent two years at *Tribune* during which time he wrote his first great masterpiece, *Animal Farm*. While working on *Animal Farm*, Orwell wrote more than 100 essays, short articles, and reviews for newspapers such as the *Manchester Evening News* and the *Observer*. He also continued his "London Letter" for the leftwing avant-garde American magazine, *Partisan Review*. It was a remarkably productive period.

Orwell had long been fascinated by a project that would show how a revolution was betrayed and fell prey to power seekers. He wrote that the idea had first come to him after his experience in the Spanish Civil War, watching the communists and their allies destroy a genuine popular revolution. He had written *Homage to Catalonia*, along with a number of essays and reviews, in which he discussed the betrayal of a revolution, but these non-fiction works hadn't reached a wide audience. Orwell was also disturbed by the slavish admiration for the Russians, and in particular, by the idolatry of Stalin during World War II.

Orwell's strategy was to sketch out his idea in the form of a beast fable, an animal fairy tale. Orwell wrote that he first conceived the idea while watching a young boy "driving a huge cart-horse along a narrow path, whipping it if tried to turn. It struck me that if only such animals became aware of their strength we should have no power over them."[74] He began to ponder what would happen if the animals used their great strength and turned it on humans.

Orwell had a fondness for animals, especially goats, and enjoyed their quirks. He and Eileen had a dog, appropriately named Marx, which Orwell trained to hunt rabbits. While living in Burma, he had maintained a small menagerie of goats, ducks, and geese. As a boy, Orwell read, and thoroughly enjoyed, fables, including those that anthropomorphized animals. Late Victorian and Edwardian England produced a rich collection of such animal stories as Kipling's *Jungle Book*, where the boy Mowgli could speak to the animals. Kenneth Grahame's *Wind in the Willows*, featuring the eccentric Toad of Toad Hall and his friends, appeared while Orwell was a schoolboy. Jacintha Buddicom wrote that Orwell particularly liked Beatrix Potter's *Pigling Bland*, in which pigs walked upright. She remembered him reading it again and again.[75]

Orwell worked assiduously for four months on *Animal Farm*, finishing it in February 1944. It is one of the most effective examples of Orwell's writing that possesses a bemused sense of humor. Shelden attributes the "wry humor" in *Animal Farm* to his wife Eileen's influence.[76] Each night he shared the latest progress of his tale with her while she would give him her reactions. According to a close friend, Lettice Cooper, who worked with her at the Ministry of Food, Eileen would fill her in the next day on the story's progress. Cooper and Eileen believed that Orwell had a winner on his hands. Orwell, who was always circumspect about his writings, confirmed their view. In a letter to Dorothy Plowman after *Animal Farm* was published, Orwell wrote that he was sorry Eileen didn't live to see his success. He wrote that she was fond of *Animal Farm*, which she "even helped in the planning of."[77]

In contrast to his other books, which he tended to denigrate as various kinds of failures, Orwell was proud of *Animal Farm*, though typically he downplayed it in a letter to the Russian literary historian Gleb Struve as "a little squib."[78] With *Animal Farm* he was seeking to reach a wider audience than he had with his past fiction and non-fiction works. Despite its brevity, just 30,000 words – really a pamphlet or a novella – Orwell knew that he had accomplished something special. In his essay "Why I Write," Orwell stated that *Animal Farm* was "the first book in which I tried, with full consciousness of what I was doing, to fuse political purpose and artistic purpose into one whole."[79]

*Animal Farm* traces what happens when a group of animals on Farmer Jones's Manor Farm revolt and seize control. With economy and wit the story perfectly allegorizes the events of the Russian Revolution from the overthrow of the Tsar to the Teheran conference among the Big Three of Churchill, Roosevelt, and Stalin in November 1943. All the key developments of the revolution are there: the revolt itself, the attempted Allied intervention, the Russian Civil War, Stalin's Five-Year Plan, the brutal purges of the mid-1930s, and more.

Orwell made the pigs the key revolutionaries, believing them to be the cleverest farm animals. The leader of the revolution, Napoleon, is modeled after Stalin. Snowball represents Trotsky, Stalin's arch enemy, while Squealer is the propaganda machine of such Communist Party news agencies as Tass and the newspaper *Pravda*. The puppies that Napoleon secretly raises, and then turns into vicious dogs, constitute the secret police – the Cheka, MVD, NKVD, KGB, etc. that terrorize the farm animals.

What made all this compelling was Orwell's ability to humanize the animals. His choices to represent each aspect of the revolution were on the mark. Thus the stolid horse Boxer was a perfect parallel to the Russian masses, who struggled to make the revolution a success and then were cruelly dispensed with.

The mare Mollie was a model for the "Whites," those Russians who fled the revolution. Many commentators believe that the cynical donkey, Benjamin, who is skeptical about the revolution, is a stand-in for Orwell. After the success of *Animal Farm*, some of his friends referred to him as "Donkey George." In a review of Arthur Koestler's novel *The Gladiators*, written while attempting to get *Animal Farm* published, Orwell argued that all revolutions in some way are failures.[80] That sense of failure and betrayal pervades *Animal Farm*.

Another aspect of *Animal Farm* unusual for Orwell's writings was his use of humor. Orwell understood the idiosyncrasies of various animals. At one point he has the cat, who he describes as disappearing whenever work had to be done, on the roof of the barn, appealing to the birds to come closer as we are all "comrades" now.

When the animals first enter Farmer Jones's house, they find hams hanging in the larder. The pigs solemnly carry the hams out and give them a formal burial.

Orwell also made fun of the Russians' embalming of Lenin. After the death of Old Major, he has the skull mounted to honor the inspiration of the revolution. This subtle dig at the communist treatment of Lenin was designed to poke fun at apologists for the revolution.

There is another scene where the pigs discover Farmer Jones's store of whisky and get drunk. The next day Squealer makes a number of public appearances, first announcing sadly that Napoleon is dying, then that he is just sick, and finally that he has miraculously recovered. It is obvious that Napoleon had a hangover. Napoleon bans the drinking of alcohol but then makes a deal with his neighbors to procure some more. When the animals discover the pigs drinking whisky, they check the Seven Commandments of Animalism that had been painted on the barn wall. The commandment "No animal should drink alcohol" now has the words "to excess" added to it.

Orwell's choice of pigs as the revolutionary cadre was a brilliant decision. Napoleon (called Caesar in the French edition, something that Orwell found revealing and humorous) perfectly captured Stalin's suspiciousness and ruthless treachery. At one point in the story Orwell shows Napoleon cowering with fear in the fight against the humans who try to re-conquer the farm. When he was informed that Stalin had actually behaved bravely during the war, Orwell rewrote the sequence.

Snowball as Trotsky was a wonderful creation. Trotsky, like Snowball, was always teeming with ideas and plans and, along with Lenin, was the real architect of the Bolshevik Revolution. Orwell has him defeated by the stolid Napoleon, who uses his bureaucratic talents to outwit his more brilliant foe. Orwell admired Trotsky as a genuine intellectual and a gifted writer, but Orwell didn't make the mistake of many leftists of believing that the revolution would have been benign if Trotsky, not Stalin, had prevailed. As a dictator, Orwell argued, Trotsky would have been preferable because "he has a much more interesting mind" than Stalin but he (and, he added, Lenin) eventually would have betrayed the revolution.[81]

This criticism of Trotsky and Lenin outraged many of Orwell's fellow leftists, who blamed Stalin for the degeneration of the revolution. However, when the Soviet archives opened after the end of the Cold War, the records indicate that Orwell was correct. In the early stages of the revolution Lenin and Trotsky engaged in brutal bloodbaths and the use of the secret police against their enemies, policies which presaged Stalin's purges of the 1930s.

After Orwell finished *Animal Farm* in March 1944 he spent a year trying to secure a publisher. His timing was bad – there was a severe wartime shortage of paper and the popularity of the Soviet Union was at its height following its great victories at Stalingrad and Kursk in 1943. The Russians had seized the offense throughout Eastern Europe, while the Western Allies had not yet invaded France and were bogged down on the Italian peninsula. Russian popularity in Great Britain was high. This was the time of the infamous "Sword of Stalingrad," a British jewel-encrusted sword created to honor Russia's triumph at the Battle of Stalingrad. The sword was placed on display in Westminster Abbey and visited by enormous crowds. Churchill presented the sword to Stalin at the Teheran conference. The entire incident disgusted Orwell as another example of what he called the power worship and blindness, especially of the English intelligentsia, toward the realities of communist tyranny.

Orwell recognized that Gollancz, who had first right of rejection to his writings, would never publish *Animal Farm* because of its devastating criticism of the Soviet Union and Stalin. He wrote Gollancz a typically forthright, albeit patronizing, letter offering him the book while warning him that it was "completely unacceptable politically from your point of view." Gollancz exercised his right to see the manuscript but wanted no part of it. He called it a general attack on an ally at a crucial time of the war. "You were right," Gollancz told Orwell, "and I was wrong," the manuscript was unacceptable given his views of the Soviet Union. For all his past criticism of the Soviet Union, Gollancz "could not bring himself to publish a satirical onslaught on its grandest panjandrum."[82]

This incident finished Gollancz in Orwell's eyes. He told his agent that he wanted no further dealings with him, as Gollancz's politics "change too fast for me."[83] Gollancz, who had a keen eye for what made a bestseller, must have regretted his refusal, especially when *Animal Farm* went on to become one of the most successful books of the twentieth century. Also, by rejecting *Animal Farm*, he lost any chance at *Nineteen Eighty-Four*, an even bigger financial success.

Thus began what D. J. Taylor has called "the saga of *Animal Farm*'s labyrinthine route to publication."[84] During the next year, at least four British publishers rejected *Animal Farm*, confirming Orwell's perception that the British intelligentsia were in the thrall of Stalin-worship.

After Gollancz, *Animal Farm* was turned down by the publishing houses of Nicolson and Watson, Jonathan Cape, Faber and Faber, and William Collins. By this time, the early summer of 1944, Orwell was getting desperate. He even talked of borrowing money from his wealthy friend David Astor to publish *Animal Farm* as a pamphlet. Orwell's friend the poet Paul Potts owned a small press, the Whitman Press, and he claims that Orwell briefly considered using it to publish *Animal Farm*.[85]

What agitated Orwell were the reasons given for rejecting *Animal Farm* – it was pure politics and had nothing to do with the literary merits of the fable. Cape, for example, argued that *Animal Farm* would be "less offensive if the predominant caste of the fable were not pigs."[86] In that way *Animal Farm* would be less likely to anger the Soviets.

Orwell found such reasoning amusing. He wrote to an old friend, the writer Inez Holden: "Imagine old Joe (who doesn't know a word of any European language) sitting in the Kremlin reading *Animal Farm* and saying, 'I don't like this.'"[87]

Orwell wouldn't have been as amused if he knew that Cape had originally decided to publish *Animal Farm* but had been dissuaded by the Ministry of Information on the grounds of not offending the Soviet Union. The official at the Ministry instrumental in pressuring Cape to reject *Animal Farm* was Peter Smollett, who was later unmasked as a Soviet spy. Interestingly enough, Orwell was suspicious of Smollett. In the list of political unreliables that he prepared for the Information Research Department in 1949, Orwell listed Smollett as "some kind of Russian agent. Very slimy person."[88]

Orwell also sent the manuscript along to T. S. Eliot, whom he deeply admired at Faber, hoping to get his approval. Eliot's reading indicates what Orwell was up against. Eliot found the tale clever and a "distinguished piece of writing," but he believed that the overall message was one of "negation." He also pointed out that *Animal Farm* was undermined by the fact that, all things considered, the pigs were the smartest animals and thus the natural leaders of the revolution. "What was needed (someone might argue) was not more communism but more public-spirited pigs."[89]

Frederic Warburg, who had published *Homage to Catalonia* when no one else would touch it, came to Orwell's rescue. He was interested in the manuscript but his press was small and suffered from a paper shortage, which plagued all publishers during the war. In July 1944, Warburg agreed to publish *Animal Farm*. It was a decision that he would never regret, as he not only got that bestseller but also *Nineteen Eighty-Four*, two of the biggest publishing successes of all time.

Despite Warburg's commitment, it took a year before *Animal Farm* finally appeared on August 17, 1945, just two days after Japan surrendered ending World War II. To the surprise of many (and the dismay of those publishers who turned it down), *Animal Farm* was a huge success. The reviews were uniformly positive. The novelist Evelyn Waugh told Orwell in a personal note that he found the story "ingenious and delightful," a reaction typical of many readers.[90] Even children could enjoy the story on its own merits. William Empson, who became a close friend to Orwell at this time, told him his young son read *Animal Farm* and the boy thoroughly enjoyed it. The writer Malcolm Muggeridge, who often lunched with Orwell, told him the same thing. That pleased Orwell.

The success of *Animal Farm* deepened the left's hatred of Orwell, which first dated from his jabs at fellow leftists in *The Road to Wigan Pier*, and from *Homage to Catalonia*, with its bitter criticism of communist perfidy in Spain. Kingsley Martin, editor of the *New Statesman*, continued his vendetta against Orwell. His reading of *Animal Farm* was typical of many of those leftists sympathetic to communism at the time. Orwell's satire showed that he had "lost faith in mankind" and that the satire was "historically false and neglectful of the complex truth about Russia."[91] None of these complex truths appeared in the *New Statesman*.

Perhaps embarrassed that he had lost out on a publishing bestseller, Gollancz expressed his disgust with *Animal Farm*. He wrote that Orwell was "much over-rated," an interesting comment given that Gollancz had discovered him and that *Animal Farm* and *Nineteen Eighty-Four* eventually sold more than 40 million copies.

The sales of *Animal Farm* surprised Warburg, who printed a first run of only 4,500 copies, which quickly sold out, and then another run of 10,000 later in the year. A further 6,000 copies sold in 1946. Even the Queen wanted a copy and dispatched a footman to find her one, which he located in an anarchist bookstore. Orwell was surprised to find that the book was being shelved in the children's section of some bookstores and he went around personally shelving it properly.

American publishers who had shown no interest in the book when Leonard Moore, Orwell's agent, tried to peddle the manuscript to them, now took notice. Dial Press, for example, had rejected *Animal Farm* out of hand on the grounds that it was "impossible to sell animal stories" in America. Harcourt Brace, a major New York firm, had a representative in London when *Animal Farm* appeared. On his recommendation and in view of its great popularity in England, Harcourt Brace decided to publish *Animal Farm* in the United States a year after its UK publication.

*Animal Farm* was published in the United States on August 25, 1946 and was a runaway bestseller when it was named a Book-of-the-Month Club selection. For the first time in his life Orwell was financially secure.

*Animal Farm* was an even greater success in America than it had been in England. By the summer of 1946, admiration for the Soviet Union had given way to the first concerns that would lead to the Cold War – a term that Orwell probably was the first to coin. Churchill had given his famous "Iron Curtain" speech in the United States in February 1946 and George Kennan's famous "Long Telegram" advocating "containment" of the Soviet Union that same year had raised doubts about Stalin's long-term goals. The first steps in developing the mental framework that soon guided Western foreign policy during the Cold War had been taken.

*Animal Farm*'s success in Great Britain and especially the United States created some confusion. Was Orwell's satire purely directed at the Soviet Union or did it possess a more universal message? American conservatives had seized on *Animal Farm* (they would also later do so with *Nineteen Eighty-Four*) as a devastating critique of communism. Dwight Macdonald, the American radical who engaged in a friendly exchange of letters with Orwell during the war, asked Orwell to clarify the message of *Animal Farm*. Orwell replied:

> Of course I intended it primarily as a satire on the Russian Revolution. But I did mean it to have a wider application in so much that I meant that that kind of revolution (violent conspiratorial revolution, led by power-hungry people) can only lead to a change of masters.[92]

Of all Orwell's writings, *Animal Farm* remains the best-loved, and, after *Nineteen Eighty-Four*, the most famous. It quickly became a staple in the English literature canon for secondary school students in Great Britain and the United States, and it was soon translated into thirty-two languages. Today that number is sixty-two. Orwell truly had succeeded in his stated aim to "fuse political purpose and artistic purpose into one whole."[93]

## Nineteen Eighty-Four

For some time Orwell had been pondering the idea of writing a novel that would show what the modern trend toward totalitarianism would look like in the future. While it is difficult to date when the idea first took hold, it appears he began thinking seriously about the theme around the time of the Teheran conference in November 1943 when the Allied leaders created new spheres of influence throughout the world – a perception that forms the closing image in *Animal Farm* of Napoleon and the human tyrants toasting one another. Orwell postponed work on *Nineteen Eighty-Four* until the summer of 1946 largely because he was busy with other writing and publishing ventures, including *Animal Farm* and his volume of *Critical Essays*. He also was involved with domestic arrangements after his wife died, finding a housekeeper and beginning his move to the island of Jura in the Hebrides.

*Nineteen Eighty-Four* was written over a two-year period, with Orwell handing in a finished copy in late November 1948. It is his most ambitious novel, a feat rendered even more impressive by the fact that he wrote much of it while in and out of sanatoria suffering from the tuberculosis that would eventually kill him.

Orwell drew on many sources for *Nineteen Eighty-Four*. He had been fascinated with utopian literature since he first read Jack London's *The Iron Heel* and H. G. Wells's novels as a young boy. Orwell continued to express interest in such books throughout his career. He was familiar with *Brave New World*, though he thought Aldous Huxley's vision of the future was too materialist with its emphasis on hedonism. Orwell was impressed by some of James Burnham's arguments about a managerial elite emerging as a ruling class in the future. He even wrote an essay-review of Burnham's influential book, *The Managerial Revolution*. In 1944 he discovered Yevgeny Zamyatin's *We* in the course of an exchange of correspondence with Gleb Struve, a specialist in Russian literature. *We* was to have more influence on *Nineteen Eighty-Four* than any other single work. Zamyatin's novel, for example, features a leader known as the Benefactor, along with analogues to Orwell's Thought Police and telescreens.

Daphne Patai argued in her book, *The Orwell Mystique*, that *Nineteen Eighty-Four* was not original. She writes that he "may have borrowed" the idea from Katherine Burdekin's novel, *Swastica Night*, which is a bit of a reach to say the least and something no other Orwell scholar believes.

Some commentators have argued that Orwell's grim portrait of the future arose from his serious illness – that is, it was a projection of a death wish. Bernard Crick and other biographers have demolished this line of thinking by noting the books and articles that Orwell was planning to write at the time of his death. They also note that Orwell's doctors mandated that he would have to live a quiet life and that he had accepted that restriction. These are hardly the responses of a man who felt doomed. He kept a notebook even while confined to bed in the hospital during his last illness in which he sketched out his ideas for projects he wanted to write – not at all the behavior of a man expecting to die.

Other writers have advanced similar arguments about the darkness of *Nineteen Eighty-Four* based on his brilliant essay "Such, Such Were the Joys," which treats the horrors of his early schooling. In his biography of Orwell, Gordon Bowker compares Winston Smith preparing to be interrogated by O'Brien to young Eric Blair sitting outside Sambo's office patiently waiting for his punishment in "Such, Such Were the Joys."[94] Peter Davison makes a powerful case that Orwell's real motivation in "Such, Such Were the Joys" was to attack the evils of private education, hoping that the Labour government would abolish such elite "public" schools.[95] Given the strictness of English libel laws, Orwell knew that his essay could not be published for years, which is another argument for believing that Orwell did not expect to die soon.

Orwell's keenest motivation for writing *Nineteen Eighty-Four* was to warn the West of certain immediate trends toward the centralization of power in the hands of a corrupt ruling class. In that respect, *Nineteen Eighty-Four* was the culmination of Orwell's thoughts on politics since he first became politically conscious around the time of *The Road to Wigan Pier*.

Orwell also was concerned by his fear that the very idea of historical truth was disappearing as the language was corrupted by the state and its propaganda organs. As a result of his experiences after he returned from Spain and found the war was distorted in the British press to serve the interests of pro-communist forces, Orwell believed that a sense of history might cease to exist in the future. What made communism a form of totalitarianism more dangerous than fascism, according to Orwell, was a simple distinction: "Hitler burned books; Stalin had them re-written."

Orwell called *Nineteen Eighty-Four* a satire. Its satirical roots can be traced back to one of Orwell's literary idols, Jonathan Swift. The novel has elements of

*Gulliver's Travels* but even more reflects Swift's savage satire, "A Modest Proposal," in which he recommended the eating of children to solve Ireland's food shortage.

*Nineteen Eighty-Four* is chosen as the date for the story because Orwell understood that the near future possessed relevance for people, unlike some distant era. People could comprehend 1984, a time many of them would live to see, while stories set hundreds or thousands of years into the future would seem irrelevant.

The world in 1984 is divided into three warring camps: Oceania, Eurasia, and Eastasia. The fighting has been going on for thirty years and has left the three societies impoverished. The issues in dispute are long forgotten and the three camps are constantly changing sides.

The physical description of the world of 1984 is simply Orwell's logical extension of the world of 1945 into a projected future: a combination of communism, Nazism, and the privations of World War II England and especially wartime London. The seedy world of Airstrip One, the England of 1984, is modeled on the bombed-out London of World War II.

The novel's protagonist is Winston Smith – the name itself is evocative: Winston for the great English statesman, and Smith, the most common of English names. Winston Smith is thirty-four years old in 1984 and works for the Ministry of Truth, where he rewrites history to suit the ever-changing party line. This allows Orwell to discuss the way that history can be distorted and revised. There are scenes where people are not only written out of history but their images in photographs disappear. This had happened in the Soviet Union where key figures in the Revolution such as Trotsky and Bukharin were simply airbrushed out of photographs. Smith's job also allows Orwell to develop one of the key themes of the novel – the concept of Newspeak, a language that the Party is creating to destroy the possibility of thinking critically. Modeled on Orwell's experience with Esperanto, and the propaganda of the war, Newspeak shows the direction Orwell feared society was heading.

Smith's very physical appearance is reminiscent of the ill Orwell at the time. It is as if Orwell looked into a mirror for his grim portrait of Smith. "The curvature of the spine was astonishing. The thin shoulders were hunched forward so as to make a cavity of the chest, a scraggy neck seemed to be doubled under the weight of the skull."[96]

Winston Smith is a member of the ruling elite's Outer Party, which allows him some privileges but no real power. Society in 1984, after thirty years of almost constant warfare, is divided into three groups: the Inner Party, which controls all power; an Outer Party of bureaucrats, and the proles; the working class, which is kept in line by gin, pornography, and sport.

Because he has vague memories of the past, Smith is discontented. He hates his job and longs for some greater meaning in his life. He is fascinated by physical reminders of the past: an old-fashioned ink pen, a notebook with rich creamy paper, and a glass paperweight – things that in themselves have no value or utility but for that very reason are dear to him. In effect, by the time the novel opens, Winston Smith is already a rebel against the ruling party and its leader, Big Brother. The first words he writes in his diary, the very possession of which is an illegal act, are DOWN WITH BIG BROTHER.

During one of Big Brother's Two-Minute Hate periods, Smith meets Julia, a beautiful young member of the Anti-Sex League. They enter into a surreptitious affair, which is illegal since the sex impulse is regarded as dangerous by the Party. For Smith, illicit sexual relations are a form of rebellion, another way of defying Big Brother. Julia, whose surname we never learn, is a generation younger than Winston, and sees sexual rebellion as a way of satisfying herself. The act itself has no political significance. The sexually liberated character of Julia resembles some of the compliant female characters of Orwell's earlier fiction – sexually available but without political awareness or conviction. This has led feminist scholars to attack Orwell for his "generalized misogyny."[97]

Winston and Julia carry on their affair in a room that Winston rents above Mr. Charrington's antique shop where Winston bought the artifacts that are illegal in Oceania. Winston tries to interest Julia in his political thought, reading to her from an illegal copy of Emmanuel Goldstein's *Theory and Practice of Oligarchical Collectivism*, the manual of the Brotherhood, the supposed revolutionary conspirators against the Party. The Goldstein character, modeled on Trotsky, may or may not exist. He may also be a creation of the Inner Party elite to entrap dissidents. Orwell defines the character of the two "rebels" in a scene where Smith is eagerly reading Goldstein in bed to Julia. She promptly falls asleep.

Orwell's emphasis on Goldstein's ideas has led some scholars to see *Nineteen Eighty-Four* as being inspired by his associations with Trotskyist groups such as the POUM or the Independent Labour Party in the past. John Newsinger, an incisive student of Orwell's political thought, believes that Orwell's contact with the American Trotskyists at the *Partisan Review*, especially such people as Dwight Macdonald, a former admirer of Trotsky, influenced Orwell's approach in *Nineteen Eighty-Four*. The evidence for this is thin. However, to Newsinger, Orwell was "a literary Trotskyist."[98]

Smith is approached by a member of the Inner Party named O'Brien, purportedly a member of the rebel Brotherhood against Big Brother. In fact, O'Brien is a member of the Thought Police and the Party's Inner Circle. Smith develops an almost dog-like loyalty to O'Brien, hanging on every word of his political philosophy.

Eventually Smith and Julia are arrested and forced to confess their disloyalty to Big Brother. The interrogation of Smith by O'Brien brings out the key theme of the novel. Smith begs O'Brien to explain what the Party's motivation really is. If you want an image of the future, O'Brien tells him, imagine a huge boot crashing down on a human face – forever.

O'Brien breaks Smith's will by placing a metal cage over his head in which a giant rat is housed, a rat being the one thing that Smith truly fears. Smith cries out, "Do it to Julia" – a symbolic betrayal of all he has professed, followed by his abject confession that he now truly loves Big Brother.

Broken and for all practical purposes a dead man, he is freed. In the penultimate scene of the novel he meets Julia in the Chestnut Café and discovers that she too betrayed him. When he returns home from the café, Smith realizes, as Orwell phrases it in the closing lines, that he "had won a victory over himself. He loved Big Brother."

Orwell submitted the manuscript of *Nineteen Eighty-Four* to Warburg in late 1948. Warburg immediately recognized that he had something special and – despite continued paper shortages during the postwar austerity period – rushed the book into print.

The book also was picked up by the American firm, Harcourt Brace, who decided to publish it at approximately the same time as the English edition appeared. The only difference at first was the title: *Nineteen Eighty-Four* in England; *1984* in the United States. When the Book-of-the-Month Club in the United States decided to adopt the novel, the editors sought to cut out material, particularly the long section on Goldstein's book and Orwell's reflections on Newspeak, the special language of Oceania. Orwell refused the cuts and threatened to cancel the contract with the Club despite the fact that it could have cost him $40,000. He told Moore that he could not "allow my book to be mucked about beyond a certain point . . ."[99] Later the Book-of-the-Month Club acceded to his wishes, leading Orwell to tell his friend Sir Richard Rees, "that virtue is its own reward, or honesty is the best policy, I forget which."[100]

*Nineteen Eighty-Four* was Orwell's greatest literary and popular success. It is also probably the most analyzed of Orwell's writings. Many aspects of *Nineteen Eighty-Four* caught the public's attention, with some readers viewing the novel as a form of prophecy, something which Orwell didn't have in mind. He was simply projecting certain trends from his own time into the near future. The prophecies or predictions were incidental to Orwell's major concerns: the loss of historical objectivity and the corruption of the language.

There was some confusion as to what Orwell was trying to say. This arose from Orwell's decision, as in *Animal Farm*, to draw heavily on the Russian experience with communism. It was easy to look at *Nineteen Eighty-Four* as an indictment of communism, with Big Brother representing Stalin and the Thought Police reflecting the Russian secret police. In truth, Orwell did draw heavily on the corruptions of the Soviet system, but he also integrated aspects of Nazism, fascism and even capitalism into his portrait of the world of 1984. He tried to clear up this confusion in the months before he died. He wrote an American union leader regarding those Americans who misinterpreted *Nineteen Eighty-Four*: "My recent novel is NOT intended as an attack on Socialism or on the British Labour Party (of which I am a supporter) but as a show-up of the perversions to which a centralized economy is liable and which have already been partly realized in Communism and Fascism."[101]

Orwell's profoundest insight is that in a totalitarian world man's life is shorn of dynamic possibilities. The end of life is completely predictable in its beginning, the beginning merely a manipulated preparation for the end. There is no opening for surprise, for that spontaneous animation which is the token of and justification for freedom. Oceanic society may evolve through certain stages of economic development, but the life of its members is static, a given and measured quality that can neither rise to tragedy nor tumble to comedy.[102]

*Nineteen Eighty-Four* was a runaway bestseller, something that genuinely surprised Orwell. It sold 50,000 copies in England and 360,000 in the United States in the first year in print. Like *Animal Farm* it continues to sell today. As the latter half of the twentieth century dawned, any doubts as to Orwell's stature as a writer of major proportions were ended. The reviews, outside the communist-influenced press, both in England and the United States were overwhelmingly enthusiastic. But all this success came too late for Orwell to enjoy it: whether he intuited it or not, he had only days left to live.

## Chapter 3

# Critical reception

## Starting out in the 1930s

Orwell's reputation as a writer in literary London began modestly. The period 1928–32 represents the writer's five years of struggle as "Eric Blair." Eager to find journalistic and reviewing assignments on his return from Burma in December 1927, he soon became a regular contributor to newspapers and magazines such as the *New English Weekly* and *Adelphi*. Scraps of biographical evidence and letters referring to lost stories with titles such as "The Sea God" and "The Man with Kid Gloves" suggest that Orwell was writing descriptive fiction (somewhat along the lines of what would later become *Burmese Days*). He wrote two novels during this time, both of which so displeased him that he destroyed them. These years witnessed only one effort of more than biographical interest, the superb, apparently autobiographical essay, "A Hanging" (1931). Yet for Etonian Orwell this was nonetheless a time of decisive déclassé experience, much of which he recast in later publications (e.g., his hop-picking and school teaching in *A Clergyman's Daughter*, and his two weeks in a Paris hospital in "How the Poor Die").

A larger work – a curious pastiche of novel, memoir, essay, and reportage – also emerged from his descent into the underworld of the transients and urban poor. Working as a *plongeur* in Paris and tramping throughout southern England, he drafted a manuscript that became his first book, *Down and Out in Paris and London*. Uncertain about its reception and anxious about how any publicity about his transient life might be received by his family, he considered at least four pen names, finally telling his publisher, Victor Gollancz, that he "rather preferred George Orwell."

So "George Orwell" was born during the early 1930s. Little known outside London literary circles in the mid-1930s, even though his first three books were also published by Harper and Brothers in America (and *Down and Out* in a French edition by Gallimard), Orwell was by no means an immediate sensation in the London literary world. He was chiefly known as an "old-fashioned" Edwardian novelist and a regular contributor (until 1935 as "Eric Blair") to the *Adelphi* and *New English Weekly*. Although Orwell continued to write reviews and short essays under the name Eric Blair, he soon came to identify with his pen name and used it exclusively within a few years.

Published in January 1933, *Down and Out* received respectful, even enthusiastic reviews. The *TLS* reviewer wrote: "It is a vivid picture of an apparently mad world that Mr. Orwell paints in his book, a world where unfortunate men are preyed upon by parasites, both insect and human, where a straight line of demarcation is drawn above which no man can hope to rise once he has fallen below its level."[1] C. Day Lewis in *Adelphi* opened his review: "Orwell's book is a tour of the underworld, conducted without hysteria or prejudice, and if the discovery of facts made any real impression on the individual conscience, the body of active reformers in this country would be inevitably increased by the number of readers of this book."[2] W. H. Davies, author of *The Autobiography of a Super Tramp*, declared in *New Statesmen and Nation* that *Down and Out* "is the kind of book I like to read, where I get the truth in chapters of real life."[3] In the US, the reviewer for *Nation* wrote:

> No writer submitting himself for the nonce to a horrible existence, for the sake of material, could possibly convey so powerful a sense of destitution and hopelessness as has Mr. Orwell, on whom these sensations were, apparently, forced. If we are correct in this conclusion, if this book is not merely a piece of "human nature faking," it is a restrained and all the more damning indictment of a society in which such things are possible.[4]

*Down and Out* was succeeded within months by Orwell's first realistic novel, *Burmese Days*. Often compared with E. M. Forster's *A Passage to India* (1927), *Burmese Days* received excellent notices on both sides of the Atlantic. Michael Sayers in *Adelphi* noted especially the "lucidity" and "transparence" of *Burmese Days*, applauding "its clarity of style, which presents the scene with the vivacity of hallucination."[5]

Cyril Connolly, in *New Statesman*, called it "a crisp, fierce, and almost boisterous attack on the Anglo-Indian." He concluded: "Personally I liked it and recommend it to anyone who enjoys a spate of efficient indignation, graphic description, excellent narrative, excitement, and irony tempered by vitriol."[6] Meanwhile, major US newspapers, such as the *New York Times Book Review* and the *Boston Evening Transcript*, gave Orwell's novel favorable notices.

A slight novel, *A Clergyman's Daughter*, appeared in 1935. Wrote Peter Quennell: "*A Clergyman's Daughter* is ambitious yet not entirely successful . . . A good deal of the writing is uncommonly forceful; but Dorothy, alas! remains a cipher. She is a literary abstraction to whom things happen . . . We have no feeling that her flight from home and her return to the rectory have any valid connection with the young woman herself."[7] In the *Observer*, L. P. Hartley wrote that "the novel's merits lie in the treatment, which is sure and bold, in the dialogue, which is always appropriate and often brilliant," but he also referred to exaggeration and strains on the reader's credulity.[8] V. S. Pritchett, in the *Spectator*, was unimpressed by the Trafalgar Square scene – "written in a stunt Joyce fashion which utterly ruins the effect."[9]

Orwell soon followed with another realistic novel, *Keep the Aspidistra Flying* (1936), which anticipated the 1950s vogue for rebel heroes and featured a semi-autobiographical "Angry Young Man" of the 1930s, Gordon Comstock. *Aspidistra* also had modest sales and received respectful reviews. Richard Rees wrote in *Adelphi*: "It makes clear that he [Orwell] is a good hater." Rees added:

> Almost everything in the modern world, from Catholicism to contraceptives he violently assaults. But beneath a rather loose violence of style there is a consistent seriousness and a real vigour which make him a more promising novelist than many whose observation is subtler and sharper. . . He has obviously a passion for writing which is quite different from the nauseous literary obsession which afflicts so many reputedly serious modern writers.[10]

## Critical controversy and popular success

During the late 1930s, Orwell became known for his reportage. Orwell increasingly invested his energies in documentary writing, both in short pieces (such as "Shooting An Elephant" [1936]) and in reportage dealing with working-class life in Britain and with the Spanish Civil War, respectively. In January 1936, Orwell was commissioned by Victor Gollancz to visit the coal mines in the north of England and share his impressions in a work to be published in the Left Book Club series.

With *The Road to Wigan Pier* (1937), Orwell's reputation quickly expanded and altered. *Wigan Pier* was selected as a Left Book Club choice for March 1937 and distributed in a Book Club edition of 43,690 copies, a hardback circulation exceeding all of Orwell's combined sales until *Animal Farm*. Within weeks of its publication, it established Orwell's reputation as a socialist critic of the left, and it soon became a subject of debate on the left and far beyond intellectual circles.

*The Road to Wigan Pier* aroused widespread comment and controversy because of its severe critique of fellow socialists. Much of the discussion on the left was, however, quite favorable. The communist Arthur Calder-Marshall began his review for *Time and Tide*: "Of Mr. Orwell's book, there is little to say except praise."[11] The *New Statesman* granted that Orwell's criticism possessed "considerable force." Douglas Goldring wrote in *Fortnightly*: "The first half of this thought-provoking book describes what the author saw in the coal areas of Lancashire and Yorkshire." He closed:

> This brilliant, disturbing book should be read and pondered over by every jobless wearer of an old school tie. Socialists who are puzzled to understand why their party has been steadily losing ground during the past ten years should read it also.[12]

Not surprisingly, a patronizing and dismissive review came from Harry Pollitt in the *Daily Worker*:

> Here is George Orwell, a disillusioned little middle-class boy who, seeing through imperialism, decided to discover what socialism has to offer. . . a late imperialist policeman . . . If ever snobbery had its hallmark placed upon it, it is by Mr. Orwell . . . I gather that the chief thing that worries Mr. Orwell is the 'smell' of the working-class, for smells seem to occupy the major portion of the book . . .. One thing I am certain of, and it is this – if Mr. Orwell could only hear what the Left Book Club circles will say about this book, then he would make a resolution never to write again on any subject that he does not understand.[13]

In early 1937 Orwell traveled to Spain where he joined the United Marxist Workers Party, or POUM, a small militia composed largely of anarchists and Trotskyists. He spent seven months in Spain, including several on the Aragon front. After getting a bullet through his windpipe that almost killed him, he wrote his childhood friend Cyril Connelly from a hospital bed in Madrid, "I have seen wonderful things, and at last I really believe in socialism."[14]

On his return to England, Orwell's personal differences with the fellow-traveling Gollancz forced him to take *Homage to Catalonia* (1938) to the new house of Secker & Warburg. As Gordon Bowker relates, when Orwell heard how few copies Warburg had sold in three months, he was horrified, and wrote asking his agent Leonard Moore to confirm the figures, hoping he had misread them. Gollancz and his friends, he now felt sure, were pressurizing papers not to review it. Though the book sold only 900 copies until its reprinting as part of the Uniform Edition in 1951, its many respectful reviews in the non-communist press enhanced Orwell's image as a leftwing journalist critical of Stalinism and as an independent-minded, if idiosyncratic, socialist.

The *Observer* called the author of *Homage to Catalonia*, "a great writer," and the *Manchester Guardian* noted the author's "fine air of classical detachment" in describing the horrors of war. John McNair, who had fought in the POUM militia alongside Orwell in Catalonia, declared in *New Leader*: "We have waited long for such a book as George Orwell's *Homage to Catalonia*. There have been many books written on the Spanish Civil War, but none containing so many, living first-hand experiences as this."[15] Philip Mairet, Orwell's editor at the *New English Weekly*, wrote:

> The book is likely to stand as one of the best contemporary documents of the struggle. Its frank individuality of outlook, combined with a certain political näiveté, gives internal evidence of its freedom from political obscurantism, for what bias it has is naked and wholly unashamed. Its literary quality, which is of a high order, is of the kind that springs from a well-extraverted attention and spontaneous reaction, so that the observations are reliable and convincingly communicated . . .
>
> This is a human book: it shows us the heart of innocence that lies in revolution; also the miasma of lying that, far more than the cruelty takes the heart out of it.[16]

Perhaps the most perceptive notice came from Orwell's recent friend, the anthropologist Geoffrey Gorer: "*Homage to Catalonia* is that phoenix, a book which is at the same time a work of first-class literature and a political document of the greatest importance." He closed:

> I have no space to dwell on the magnificent literary qualities of the book, its brilliant descriptions of Catalan landscape, of the emotional atmosphere of a revolutionary militia, of Barcelona in different phases, the vividness of the accounts of fighting in the trenches and in the streets, the account of being wounded almost to death, of being hunted like a criminal. Emphatically, this is a book to read, politically and as literature it is a work of first-class importance. It will probably be abused both by Conservatives and Communists; anyone interested in the political

situation (whatever their own views) or in literature would be foolish to neglect it.[17]

> We could be like him if we surrendered a little of the cant that comforts us, if for a few weeks we paid no attention to the little group with which we habitually exchanged opinions, if we took our chance of being wrong or inadequate, if we looked simply and directly ... [He] liberates us ... He frees us from the need for the inside dope. He implies that our job is not to be intellectual, certainly not intellectual in this sense or that, but merely to be intelligent according to our lights. He restores the old sense of the democracy of the mind ... He has the effect of making us believe that we may become full members of the society of thinking men. That is why he is a figure for us.[18]

Orwell's reputation grew more slowly during the war years. Just weeks before fighting broke out in September 1939, he published his fourth and final realistic novel of the decade, *Coming Up for Air*. Although it did no better commercially than his earlier fiction, the *TLS* made it a recommended novel of the week, and it too received mostly favorable notices. The *TLS* reviewer proclaimed: "Mr. Orwell writes with hard, honest clarity and unswerving precision of feeling."[19] *The Times* of London heralded it as the answer to "one of the age's puzzles – the cult of the little man." On home turf, Orwell's colleague Winfred Horrabin wrote in *Tribune*: "In a hundred novels the life and thought of our time is being expressed and, as in George Orwell's latest and in many ways best work, as finely expressed as in an accurate photograph."[20]

*Coming Up* marked not only Orwell's farewell to the realistic novel, but also a temporary shift away from fiction altogether. As *Time and Tide*'s film and theatre reviewer (1940–41) and a BBC talks producer for India (1941–43), Orwell found less time for what he considered "serious" writing and turned more to journalism and the critical essay. During these years, his major work of criticism – which included three of his most famous essays (on Dickens, Henry Miller, and boys' newspapers) – was *Inside the Whale* (1940).

Reviewing the collection, critics lavished their praise. Arthur Calder-Marshall in *Time and Tide* began: "Must read. Three essays, Dickens, Boy's Weeklies, Henry Miller. Brilliant writer. Superb."[21] In the *New English Weekly*, Philip Mairet delivered more kudos: "There is no English writer of today whose words come better off the page and into the mind than those of George Orwell." Mairet concluded:

> Orwell is one of the contemporary writers best worth having: he lives to learn, he knows something about the society he lives in, he has courage and, as this books shows, a progressive faculty for criticism. The value of such writers is comparable to that of certain brain-cells to the body;

society needs them to keep it's consciousness. Also to keep an intelligence free – in his own words – from [quoting Orwell's famous closing line in the Dickens essay] "all the smelly little orthodoxies which are now contending for our souls."[22]

Likewise, the *TLS* reviewer, though voicing skepticism about the literary value of Miller's writings, concluded: "One is impressed by Mr. Orwell's effort to come clean and maintain a blunt and tenacious honesty of mind."[23] Max Plowman, Orwell's editor-friend at *Adelphi*, declared admiringly:

> And it is in his intense perception of the lie that George Orwell becomes a great writer. He sees it with unique clarity because his whole attitude, both social and political, is that of a man who knows that common decency is fundamental to any tolerable state of existence, and that without the immediate recognition of it as basic, all chatter about liberty and equality is mere intellectual vapour.[24]

A quirky review from Q. D. Leavis in *Scrutiny* closed with a suggestion that, as it were, he switch professional careers to her own line of work: "If he would give up trying to be a novelist Mr. Orwell might find his *métier* in literary criticism, in a special line of it peculiar to himself and which is particularly needed now."[25]

Orwell returned from Spain a changed man – a convinced democratic socialist and a writer committed to the realization of a socialist utopia in Britain. In *The Lion and the Unicorn* (1941), Orwell envisioned a form of "revolutionary war socialism" that would transform bourgeois England into a more egalitarian, democratic socialist nation. Reviewing the book, the *Listener* greeted it enthusiastically, arguing that a truly egalitarian socialist state was "an idea upon which many who do not call themselves socialists can unite, first to win the war, and then to create a new society."[26] While expressing reservations about much of Orwell's political analysis, V. S. Pritchett placed Orwell as both a rebel and stylist in the distinguished company of Cobbett and Defoe. Pritchett concluded: "He writes in a lucid conversational style which wakens one up suddenly like cold water dashed in the face."[27] *The Lion and the Unicorn* was also Orwell's first book to attract the notice of the *Partisan Review* writers in New York, for whom Orwell had just begun to contribute his regular "London Letter." Wrote Dwight Macdonald in *Partisan Review*: "There is also a *human* quality to Orwell's political writing; you feel it engages him as a moral and cultural whole, which our own Marxist epigones seem to feel is somehow sinful." Like Pritchett, Macdonald was also not without reservations about Orwell's political stance. Macdonald concluded:

Perhaps the clue to this odd combination of acuteness as an observer and infantilism as a theorist may be found in Orwell's general intellectual orientation. He reacts so violently against the admittedly great defects of the leftwing intellectual tradition of the last two decades as to deny himself as an intellectual.[28]

By 1942, Orwell's hopes for a political revolution had dimmed, and he began working at the BBC as a broadcaster to the Indian subcontinent. While at the BBC Orwell began to compose *Animal Farm*, whose aim (as he later explained in the preface to the Ukrainian translation) was to "destroy the myth that Russia is a socialist country." Completed in late 1944, it was rejected by more than two dozen publishers in Britain and the US (including by T. S. Eliot at Faber).

Yet historical conditions were changing and the tide of events was moving in Orwell's direction. He was a "premature anti-Stalinist," a phrase formerly used as a smear by hostile leftists that soon would represent a badge of honor. However, early postwar geopolitical events caused the remaining Red-tinted scales to fall from the eyes of Western intellectuals.

As we saw in our discussion of *Animal Farm* in the previous chapter, concern about wartime ally Russia, along with Secker & Warburg's shortage of paper, delayed the book's publication more than seventeen months after Orwell's February 1944 completion date. (Several English publishers and a dozen or more American publishers turned down *Animal Farm* on political grounds. One American house, Dial Press, innocently mistook the fable for "an animal story.") Finally published in August 1945 by Secker & Warburg and August 1946 by Harcourt, Brace, *Animal Farm* was selected as a September 1946 Book-of-the-Month Club choice.

*Animal Farm* exploded on the cultural front with an impact comparable to the dropping of the atom bombs on Hiroshima and Nagasaki. It embodied what many postwar conservatives, centrists, and anti-communist liberals came to believe about "Uncle Joe" Stalin. Its publication (shortly after V-J Day) transformed Orwell's postwar reputation internationally almost as suddenly and decisively as had *The Road to Wigan Pier* within the British left a decade earlier. In the year after its American publication in 1946, it went through nine printings in Britain and sold more than a half-million copies in the US.

The fable not only enhanced Orwell's reputation in intellectual circles. It also made him a widely popular author. The *Spectator* reviewer, W. J. Turner, said *Animal Farm* exposed "a colossal deception" and was "calculated to drive the amateur Bolsheviks of Battersea, East Aldgate and Mayfair into a frenzy of rage."[29] In *Horizon*, Connolly wrote famously: "[He] is a revolutionary who is in love with 1910." Connolly went on:

> Never before has a progressive political thinker been so handicapped by
> nostalgia for the Edwardian shabby-genteel or the under-dog.
> Nevertheless, *Animal Farm* is one of the most enjoyable books since the
> war, it is deliciously written, with something of the feeling, the
> penetration and the verbal economy of Orwell's master, Swift.[30]

One of the few dissents from the chorus was sounded by Orwell's bête noire at
the *New Statesman*, Kingsley Martin, who read *Animal Farm* as a simplistic
Trotskyite bromide, arguing that Orwell's naïve fairy tale about USSR history
would have had a happy ending "if the wicked Stalin had not driven the brave
and good Trotsky out of Eden."[31]

As for Orwell's non-fiction, it continued to be highly regarded in England and
increasingly so in America. As a result of his regular "As I Please" *Tribune*
column (1943–47) and *Observer* war reports (1945), Orwell became known
outside the London intelligentsia as a journalist. With his bi-monthly "London
Letter" in *Partisan Review* (1941–46), Orwell became well known during this
time in New York intellectual circles. His name became linked in America with
anti- and ex-communist European socialists, including Spender, Koestler,
Silone, Gide, Malraux, Victor Serge, and Franz Borkenau, all of whom Orwell
either met or praised in print. His essays after *Inside the Whale* during the war
years (on penny postcards, thriller fiction, Wells, Dalí, and P. G. Wodehouse)
further established him as an essayist of distinction and made clear his serious
interest in popular culture.

Urged by his publishers, Orwell collected these and other wartime essays
into a second volume of literary and cultural criticism that he published in late
March 1945, just weeks before *Animal Farm*. Influential Anglo-American
reviewers (Pritchett, Eric Bentley, Joseph Wood Krutch) hailed Orwell's
*Critical Essays* (American title: *Dickens, Dali and Others*) enthusiastically.
Although Evelyn Waugh, an outspoken Catholic apologist and devout believer,
expressed regret that Orwell's essays lacked the "religious sense," Waugh
nonetheless concluded: "They represent at its best the new humanism of the
common man ... there is nothing in his writing that is inconsistent with high
moral principles."[32] V. S. Pritchett called Orwell "a kind of Kipling turned
upside down" whose "traditions ... are those of the Right, and he cannot quite
forgive the world for driving him to the Left." Pritchett pronounced Orwell's
essays, "brilliant examples of political anthropology applied to literature by a
nonconforming mind."[33] The philosopher Stuart Hampshire lauded Orwell's
catholicity of mind, suggesting that Orwell's essay collection would appeal both
to a mass audience as well as to intellectuals: "Almost everybody who reads it
will enjoy it and be stimulated by it; it is easily and forcefully written, and, in

addition to its intellectual brilliance, has all the qualifications for great popularity – including a barely concealed impatience with highbrows and a suggestion of insularity. Nevertheless, high-brows will enjoy it most."[34] Writing from the US, Eric Bentley agreed: "And it has driven him to adopt a splendid forthrightness of manner; his style is a model for all who would write simply and forcefully. I hope they stimulate American critics to analyze the comic-strips and the pulps. The brilliance of Mr. Orwell's pioneer effort should put them on their mettle."[35] Speaking for the New York intellectual community in *Partisan Review*, Newton Arvin added: "Orwell's critical work is too humane at its core and too salutary in its main effects not to elicit a sense of gratitude."[36]

As his health worsened, Orwell set about composing a kind of follow-up to *Animal Farm*. He described it as "a fantasy written in the form of an anti-utopia." Originally entitled *The Last Man in Europe*, it was published in June 1949 under the title *Nineteen Eighty-Four*. The book was welcomed by leading critics in both Britain and America. Particularly innovative was Orwell's satirical treatment of Basic English, which he called Newspeak. Like *Animal Farm*, *Nineteen Eighty-Four* also received a powerful boost as a July 1949 choice of the Book-of-the-Month Club. "Great Books Make Themselves," proclaimed the August 1949 *Book-of-the-Month Club News*, in a headline running over ecstatic tributes from Bertrand Russell, Arthur Schlesinger, Jr., and others.

Nothing, of course, could have been wider of the mark than the headline's declaration, for *Nineteen Eighty-Four* – whatever its literary merits – was (like *Animal Farm*) the beneficiary of a powerful (if largely unorganized) campaign to boost it by prominent opinion makers, influential publications, and leading cultural institutions. The imprimatur of the literary establishment came from Harold Nicolson in the *Observer*, who declared the "Inferno atmosphere" "cunningly created and well maintained" and found the whole book "impressive." V. S. Pritchett, in the *New Statesman*, dubbed Orwell "a great pamphleteer" and saw the hand of the religious dissident behind the novel. "He is like some dour Protestant or Jansenist who sees his faith corrupted by the 'doublethink' of the Roman Catholic Church, and who fiercely rejects the corrupt civilizations that appear to be able to flourish even under this dispensation."[37]

In the US, Philip Rahv, the co-editor of *Partisan Review*, wrote in his magazine: "It can be said of Orwell that he is the best kind of witness, the most reliable and scrupulous. This is far and away the best of Orwell's books." Rahv added:

> As a narrative it has tension and actuality to a terrifying degree; still it will not do to judge it primarily as a literary work of art. Like all Utopian

literature, from Sir Thomas More and Campanella to William Morris, Bellamy and Huxley, its inspiration is scarcely such as to be aesthetically productive of ultimate or positive significance...*Nineteen Eighty-Four* chiefly appeals to us as a work of the political imagination, and the appeal is exercised with gravity and power.

This novel is the best antidote to the totalitarian disease that any writer has so far produced. Everyone should read it; and I recommend it particularly to those liberals who still cannot get over the political superstition that while absolute power is bad when exercised by the Right, it is in its very nature good and a boon to humanity once the Left, that is to say "our own people," takes hold of it.[38]

Not all reviewers were so laudatory. Predictably, pro-Stalinist critics were hostile. Although he had written an appreciative notice of *The Road to Wigan Pier* and a rave review of *Inside the Whale*, Arthur Calder-Marshall in *Reynolds News* derided Orwell's association with POUM, and castigated *Animal Farm*, which "brought him a fortune from reactionaries in this country and the USA." *Nineteen Eighty-Four* "will be used as election propaganda by the Tories" he concluded, adding: "The sooner Comrade Orwell assumes the penname of Eric Blair, the better. Except, of course, that Mr. Blair, ex-Etonian, ex-civil servant, had no literary reputation at all."[39]

[I]n describing a most monstrous future in store for man, he imputes every evil to the people. He is obliged to admit that in 1984 . . . capitalism will cease to exist, but only for opening the way to endless wars and the degradation of mankind, which will be brought down to the level of robots called "proles"... But the people are not frightened by any such fears of instigators of a new war. The people's conscience is clearer today than ever before. The foul maneuvers of mankind's enemies become more understandable every day to millions of common people.[40]

## Posthumous fame

The leading literary and political intellectuals mourned Orwell's passing in January 1950. In his *Observer* obituary, Arthur Koestler said, "To meet one's favourite author in the flesh is mostly a disillusioning experience. George Orwell is one of the few writers who looked and behaved exactly as the reader expected him to look and behave ... The urge of genius and the promptings of common sense can rarely be reconciled; Orwell's life was a victory of the former over the latter."[41] Stephen Spender called him "an Innocent, a kind of English Candide of the twentieth century ... He was perhaps the least Etonian character who has ever come from Eton."[42] V. S. Pritchett famously pronounced Orwell "the wintry conscience of a generation" and "an Old School Tie [who] had 'gone native in his own country.'"[43] Bertrand Russell lamented: "His personal life was tragic, partly owing to illness, but still more owing to a love of humanity and an incapacity for comfortable illusion ... I find in men like Orwell the half, but only the half, of what the world needs; the other half is still to seek."[44] Wrote E. M. Forster:

> Many critics besides Orwell are fighting for the purity of prose and deriding officialese, but they usually do so in a joking off-hand way, and from the aesthetic stand-point. He is unique in being immensely serious, and in connecting good prose with liberty. George Orwell will be read for a long time to come, but for a reason which might not have much pleased him – namely, that he is such splendid entertainment. His themes are usually distressing, but somehow his valiant treatment of them sends our spirits up.[45]

In the five postwar years before his death, Orwell had also been taken up by the American literary intelligentsia. The critical elite in New York decided that his brand of liberal-radical politics and his bracing anti-utopian fantasies were ideally suited to their literary and ideological purposes. They admired Orwell as one of their own, a radical anti-Stalinist and brilliant leftwing pamphleteer. Soon the younger members of their group (such as Irving Howe) would also come to regard him as a kind of intellectual big brother, to whom they could look for guidance. American intellectuals such as Lionel and Diana Trilling, Philip Rahv, and Irving Howe associated with *Partisan Review* and *Commentary*, were crucial for establishing a critical consensus that prepared the way for Orwell's wider reputation to develop. By the early 1950s, partly as a result of their critical endorsement, *Animal Farm* and *Nineteen Eighty-Four* became institutionalized both in American and British school curricula. They became required reading for junior and senior high school students in the US (and, in Britain, in GCSE and A-level classes).

Both the perceived split in Orwell's reputation between the man and the works and the view of Orwell as a "saint" emerged full-blown soon after his death. The former crystallized almost immediately upon the appearance of *Nineteen Eighty-Four*. The latter image took shape starting with the acclamatory obituaries of the man from Koestler, Pritchett, and other acquaintances. In the wake of the success of *Animal Farm* and *Nineteen Eighty-Four*, Harcourt, Brace had scheduled an early 1950 publication date for the first American editions of Orwell's early works. By coincidence these books (*Down and Out, Burmese Days, Coming Up for Air*) were published in the month of Orwell's death. So fresh was the image of the man in critics' minds that reviews of these works more closely resembled new obituary tributes. In June 1950 *The World Review* devoted a special number to Orwell, featuring excerpts from his wartime diaries and more praise from acquaintances such as Muggeridge, Spender, Bertrand Russell, and Tom Hopkinson. The essay collection *Shooting an Elephant* appeared later that same year, bringing yet another round of reminiscences and salutes. Soon Harcourt, Brace issued American editions of *Homage to Catalonia* (1952) and *Keep the Aspidistra Flying* (1956), along with a 1953 essay collection, *Such, Such Were the Joys* (UK title: *England Your England*). Commenting on Orwell's ascension in a review of these collections in the mid-1950s, when his style and ethos had become the model for literary groups such as the "Movement" writers and the so-called Angry Young Men, Henry Popkin wrote from America in *Kenyon Review*: "We praise the honest, angry man revealed in these essays more even than the essays that reveal the man."[46]

> In the Britain of the Fifties, along every road that you moved, the figure of Orwell seemed to be waiting. If you tried to develop a new kind of popular culture analysis, there was Orwell, if you wanted to report on work of ordinary life, there was Orwell; if you engaged in any kind of socialist argument, there was an enormously inflated statue of Orwell warning you to go back. Down into the Sixties political editorials would regularly admonish younger radicals to read their Orwell and see where all that led to.[47]

Orwell's popular reputation also continued to climb in the 1950s. The first event that launched it into the stratosphere was the BBC TV adaptation of *Nineteen Eighty-Four* in December 1954. Viewed on three successive Sundays by the largest audience to that date in BBC TV history, a total of more than 16 million viewers, *Nineteen Eighty-Four* surged from a respectable sales figure of 150 copies per week to more than 2,000 per day. It maintained that rate for months and thereafter sold on average more than 300,000 copies per year in the US and Britain. Both *Animal Farm* and *Nineteen Eighty-Four* also entered school curricula not only in Britain and America, but also in many countries of the British Commonwealth at this time.

After *Animal Farm* and *Nineteen Eighty-Four* had been taken up by the Book-of-the-Month Club, they were soon translated into numerous languages, owing partly to the fact that they were surreptitiously sponsored by the CIA and by MI6, the British equivalent. It is a little-known fact that Orwell's last two books have sold more than any other pair of serious novels by any other author in history – more than 50 million copies in sixty-two languages, partly because of the backing of the CIA, whose agents also convinced Orwell's widow to sign over the film rights of *Animal Farm* and *Nineteen Eighty-Four* in the mid-1950s. The CIA thereupon cleverly authorized adaptations of *Animal Farm* and *Nineteen Eighty-Four* with two different endings. For those English-speaking and/or Western countries familiar with Orwell's work, the ending in conformity with the book was used. However, in the Third World and Eastern Europe, a very different set of endings was shot.

Orwell's fable ends with the pigs with full control as Napoleon boasts that *Animal Farm* is now more tyrannical than even Manor Farm under Farmer Jones had been. In other words, Stalinism is even worse than Czarism under Nicholas II. However, in the CIA's adaptation released in the Third World and in Eastern Europe, the ending was changed. Instead Boxer, the representative of the working class, leads a march of the animals to the farm house, in which Napoleon and the other pigs now reside. And just as Napoleon with the other pigs is toasting his success, Boxer's brigade tramples and destroys the manor. The message was clear: "Don't give up against Stalinism, don't be content with 'containment.' Roll back Stalinism! Push the communists out of Eastern Europe and defeat them in the propaganda battle in the Third World!" The film aimed to inspire dissidents against Stalinism after the East Berlin uprising in June 1953 had been ruthlessly and effectively suppressed when the Russian tanks rolled in.

The film version of *Nineteen Eighty-Four* would attempt to do the same at the time of the Hungarian rebellion in 1956. The novel ends in Room 101, with Winston having been brainwashed by O'Brien. The last line of *Nineteen Eighty-Four* reads: "He loved Big Brother." However, in the movie version, Winston and Julia are firing round after round of machine artillery against the Thought Police agents. Only in the last moment do this brave couple fall as heroic victims. But the message again is: "Don't give up, it all depends on you, and you can succeed."

The impact of the CIA sponsorship for the development of Orwell's sudden international reputation, especially outside the English-speaking world, cannot be overstated. Largely because the British and American foreign intelligence services, including the CIA, began distributing *Animal Farm* and *Nineteen Eighty-Four* (and even some of Orwell's other works) throughout the world and sponsored major film adaptations of his last two books, Orwell metamorphosed from a nearly unknown author in 1944 to a world-renowned author in dozens of languages within a decade. Without their sponsorship of the translation, adaptation, and distribution of his work, it is unlikely that Orwell could have become known so widely and so quickly – the 1954 BBC TV sensation notwithstanding. His meteoric rise in reputation owed not just to a favorable, adventitious connection with the *Zeitgeist* (though it was partly that); it was also due to the very deliberate promotion of Orwell's work by the intelligence services to wage a cold war of words.

Beginning in the late 1950s, Orwell's reputation underwent a decade of distancing, revision, and reconsolidation. The Orwell industry suffered a mild recession. Orwell's prominence in the media declined noticeably and his public reputation dipped accordingly. As the Cold War entered a new and calmer phase, Orwell's best-known works, *Animal Farm* and *Nineteen Eighty-Four*, lost their immediacy for the media and for many readers.

In America, Orwell's popular reputation faded after 1956, but his critical standing remained high. Because many of Orwell's books published in America in the early 1950s were US first editions, most American readers had not known the man, and so from the start they had looked primarily at the writings, or at the man in the writings. American academics began writing scholarly articles and books on Orwell, sometimes claiming this distance as an advantage. American readers had not identified with Orwell to the extent of his English contemporaries and younger English intellectuals; no disillusion with and devaluation of Orwell thus occurred in the US to match the British reaction.

The year 1968 was a momentous one not only for the world but also for Orwell's reputation. The publications of *Collected Essays, Journalism, and Letters of George Orwell* (*CEJL*, 1968) that year, followed during the next decade by the two-volume biography by Peter Stansky and William Abrahams (*The Unknown Orwell*, 1972; *Orwell: The Transformation*, 1979), renewed critical interest in the man, especially in his prewar years. Even a play was written in 1976 dramatizing Orwell's life, *Outside the Whale*, by Stephen Holman. (Another dramatization of Orwell's life, *Eric Blair Tonight*, by Howard Slaughter, was performed in January 1984 at the University of Akron, Ohio.)

*CEJL* contained most of Orwell's major essays, a majority of the *Tribune* columns, and many other forgotten short pieces (though there were some significant omissions). Although *CEJL* did not settle any disputes about Orwell's work, it provided a more rounded picture of Orwell's life and enabled scholars to understand his development better. It also exposed the thinness of much of the pre-1968 Orwell criticism, which had usually been based only on the fiction and already collected essays.

Both Orwell's aging friends and younger critics raved about the volumes. Wrote Malcolm Muggeridge:

> I have always thought that Orwell, apart from anything else, was the perfect twentieth-century stylist. His dry sentences with their splendid

clarity and smoldering indignation convey better than any other
contemporary writer the true mood of our times. He stood alone in every
sense, but especially in the temper of his mind . . . I think his journalism
was his best work and when I say *his* best I mean *the* best.[48]

Anthony Powell concurred, and he closed with an intriguing counterfactual
proposition about Orwell's pen name: *CEJL* "prompts the fascinating spec-
ulation about what would have happened if – as he at one moment suggested –
Orwell had called himself 'H. Lewis Allways.'"[49] Voicing the sentiments of his
generation of New York intellectuals, Irving Howe declared: "For a whole
generation – mine – Orwell was an intellectual hero . . . More than any other
English intellectual of our age, he embodied the values of personal independ-
ence and a fiercely democratic radicalism."[50]

> We tend all too easily to lose sight of the human dimension of reputation. For it is not
> just literary achievement that we are discussing here, but the relationship among
> people. Orwell's admirers have had a personal, not merely a literary, relationship
> with him; in particular, his colleagues and friends experienced not just the man in the
> writings, but the man in the flesh. They also periodically met after Orwell's death and
> renewed their memories of the man. They and Orwell once worked together,
> lunched together, drank together, argued, laughed, commiserated. Reputation
> emerges not only from literary response, but also from human interaction. It is not
> abstracted faces and images we are examining, but ways of seeing, modes of
> receiving, forms of imagining Orwell by unique human beings. The fabric of repu-
> tations is dyed the color of our lives.[51]

As the Anglo-American left entered a new phase of radical politics, *CEJL*
also became a subject of political debates in the late 1960s. Wrote Conor Cruise
O'Brien:

> It would be a pity if the present younger generation, which could and
> should learn from him how to write English, were to remain cut off from
> him by assurances that he was a dedicated anti-communist . . . What
> should be remembered is the free, candid, often mistaken mind of a man
> who asserted and defended human decency: a more disconcerting
> enterprise than he originally reckoned it to be.[52]

George Steiner also reflected on Orwell's contemporary relevance: "To me,
the notion of 'reviewing' George Orwell is mildly impertinent. Anyone who
earns his living writing about books and politics, who tries to get the words on
the page aligned cleanly, so that the light can get through, finds himself in a
special relationship to Orwell." Steiner went on to predict that Orwell would
have had no truck with the New Left:

The failure of the 'new left' (why 'new'?) to link its critique of the Vietnam war with any responsible plan for an alternative policy would have drawn Orwell's fire. To orate fluently about American atrocities and pass over those of the Vietcong, to advocate withdrawal without tackling such political, human realities as the fate of several million refugees from the North – these postures would have struck Orwell with ironic familiarity. The divorcement between mental agility and a capacity to take political action seemed to him the besetting sin of the liberal conscience, as did the habit of abstraction, of simplification, in the face of realities which are messy and irrational. One can hear him saying, the day after the Soviet invasion of Prague, that this latest spasm of the Stalinist terror, which he fought his whole life, might never have happened had the West not rearmed NATO Germany or had we dealt, using a minimum of common sense, with the problem of the status of East Germany. What need there is, just now, of an Orwell essay on the wholly understandable but probably self-betraying and self-defeating course of Israeli politics and policy! Everywhere, since Guernica and Madrid, the lies have thickened and barbarism has drawn closer.[53]

## "Countdown" to 1–9–8–4

The lull in Orwell's reputation that occurred after it had skyrocketed in the mid-1950s was followed by a second great moment of reputation-building in the early 1980s: the so-called 1984 countdown. During the autumn of 1983 and the spring of 1984, Orwell's dystopia achieved the unprecedented feat of reaching Number One on the *New York Times* bestseller list, where it stayed for weeks. No bygone book – let alone a novel originally published thirty-five years earlier – had ever returned to bestseller status at this level. Nor was the phenomenon limited to book sales. TV documentaries, specials devoted to Orwell, and a new adaptation of *Nineteen Eighty-Four* (starring Richard Burton as O'Brien and John Hurt as Winston) were all part of the "Orwellmania" craze during 1983–84.

During the early 1980s, Orwell's reputation ballooned and ascended into the literary firmament and cultural stratosphere. Bernard Crick's long-awaited, authorized biography, *George Orwell: A Life* (1980), cleared up much of the confusion about Orwell's early career. But it upset Sonia Orwell and some old Orwell friends (Rayner Heppenstall, George Woodcock) with its purported inaccuracies and "lifeless" portrait of the man; and some conservative intellectuals (Norman Podhoretz, Leopold Labedz) with its allegedly partisan leftist stance.

The 1984 "countdown" – the word itself a culminating product of several years of reputation-building – discernibly began shortly after Crick's biography appeared. Attention not only to *Nineteen Eighty-Four* but also to George Orwell and his entire oeuvre increased dramatically. During 1983 and 1984, what the mass media called "Orwellmania" spurred *Nineteen Eighty-Four* alone to sales of almost 4 million copies.

Although the decade from the mid-1980s to the mid-1990s witnessed no sharp dip in Orwell's reputation to compare with the late 1950s and early 1960s, it was inevitable that the hubbub occasioned by the "countdown to 1984" would eventually die down and that interest in Orwell would gradually subside from its high-water mark of the mid-1980s. This turned out to be particularly the case in the mass media. Still, the 1990s witnessed a few significant film productions of Orwell's work, including Nick Danzinger's *Down and Out* (1993) and Robert Beirman's film adaptation of *Keep the Aspidistra Flying* (1997). Much discussed was Ken Loach's film, *Land and Freedom: The Revolution Betrayed* (1995), whose subtitle owes to Leon Trotsky's masterwork and which addresses the same themes as *Animal Farm*.

Although Orwell's public prominence in the media declined after the "Orwellmania" of 1983–84, scholarly and intellectual reappraisals of his work did not follow the tendency in the early 1950s toward a downward revaluation *en bloc*. Nor did a division between British and American judgments emerge. Rather, the Orwell cottage industry continued to hum along. The biggest publishing event was the appearance of the first several volumes of Peter Davison's edition of *The Complete Works of George Orwell* in 1986–87. These volumes included expurgated passages from selected Orwell novels (e.g., a rape scene in *A Clergyman's Daughter*) and a new nine-volume *CEJL* featuring hundreds of letters and journalistic pieces omitted from the 1968 *CEJL*.

New primary material was also uncovered in Britain and America. More than ninety letters were found at Indiana University, apparently sold at auction in the early 1950s and since then forgotten. William West also discovered 62 radio scripts and 250 Orwell letters misfiled in the BBC archives. This material was later published in two volumes, accompanied by inflated claims as to its significance, as *The War Broadcasts* (1985) and *The War Commentaries* (1986).

Among the Orwell criticism to appear during this period was John Rodden's *The Politics of Literary Reputation* (1989), which was the first systematic historical and sociological study of Orwell's reputation. In the early 1990s, William West followed his two books of the 1980s with *Nineteen Eighty-Four: The Truth Behind the Satire* (1992), and Stephen Ingle explored Orwell's legacy to British socialism in *George Orwell: A Political Life* (1993).

As the end of the millennium approached, a British bookseller, Waterstones, asked its customers to list the one hundred greatest books of the twentieth century. J. R. R. Tolkien's *The Lord of the Rings* ranked first, followed by Orwell's two classic studies of totalitarianism, *Nineteen Eighty-Four* and *Animal Farm*. More than a half-century after his death, Orwell was more widely read than any of his English contemporaries or successors.

A consensus had also formed among intellectuals and in the literary academy that Orwell's last two books had constituted a type of psychological "deterrence" on the cultural front during the Cold War era. As Alvin Kernan summed it up in a memoir about his early postwar student years published in 1999, which coincided with the fiftieth anniversary of the appearance of *Nineteen Eighty-Four*:

> We certainly, unlike earlier and later generations of students, had no thought that American capitalism was irredeemably corrupt or that communism and Soviet Russia offered any hope whatsoever in the future. Our attitudes toward communism were pretty much formed by two great literary attacks of our time on that system, Arthur Koestler's *Darkness at Noon* (1941) and George Orwell's *Animal Farm* (1946). These two books, along with Orwell's later *Nineteen Eighty-Four* (1949), may well have been as effective in the Cold War as were containment and nuclear deterrence. Certainly they convinced my generation that whatever was wrong, communism was not going to make it better – in fact it would make it worse.[54]

Not a single [Western journalist] has had the wisdom, the courage, or the honesty to acknowledge at long last that George Orwell with his prophetic gift diagnosed the syndrome of present-day capitalism with which we must co-exist today for lack of something better, restraining with all our might its pathologically militaristic, nuclear-missile ambitions.[55]

Yet all these achievements belonged to the twentieth century – and thus to the past. This huge public renown arguably owed to the unique historical and political conditions that had launched "Orwell" into the international stratosphere, indeed especially to the two "volcanic" moments in Orwell's reception history: the Cold War hysteria of the 1950s and the *Nineteen Eighty-Four* countdown.[56] However much the Orwell centenary might generate another bubble in his reputation, his outsized public image appeared inevitably destined to shrink radically.

Nor was this expectation surprising: indeed, John Rodden wrote in *The Politics of Literary Reputation* that he did "not expect the Orwell centennial in 2003 to be more than an academic affair." That prediction turned out to be largely true. But Orwell did not go down the memory hole. Just the reverse. Admittedly, no "countdown to 2003" transpired to match the countdown frenzy that began in 1982 (if not earlier) and continued well past New Year's Day, 1984. Yet both Orwell and "Orwell" re-emerged in the late 1990s and during the run-up to 2003 as headliners. For instance, launched in the late 1990s, the UK television program *Big Brother* entered new international markets in 2002–3 and was alluded to incessantly in 2003 as Orwell's birthday approached.

## Orwell in the twenty-first century

The third and final crescendo in Orwell's astonishing afterlife occurred during 2002–3, during the run-up to the centennial of his birth. Between 2000 and 2003, four new biographies of Orwell appeared and the biggest international conference ever devoted to him was also staged, along with a new opera of *Nineteen Eighty-Four* and numerous documentaries.

This decade of 1997–2007 also witnessed a spate of commemorations and retrospectives on Orwell in the media, along with new adaptations of his books. Most important among the latter was the October 1999 broadcast by Turner Network Television, with great Shakespearean actors such as Patrick Stewart (Napoleon) and Peter Ustinov (Old Major) providing the animal voices and a cutting-edge voice-tech firm furnishing the combination live-action and animated effects. The new adaptation merges computer graphics, humans, animals, and what is termed in the animated film industry "animatronics," which are animal robot "doubles" who possess human voices. While such high-tech puppetry and computer effects had already been used to stunning ends in *Babe* (1995), and *Babe: Pig in the City* (1998), the *Animal Farm* adaptation incorporated more advanced technological innovations that rendered it a major breakthrough in cinematography.

On the small screen, a segment of Simon Schama's award-winning broadcast, *The History of Britain: The Fate of Empire*, paired the two Winstons (Churchill and Smith), comparing Sir Winston Churchill and Orwell as the two great architects of the twentieth century. First aired in June 2002, it cast them as Emersonian "representative men," with Churchill the representative man of action and Orwell the representative man of reflection. Among the other media tributes to Orwell in 2002–3 were an award-winning PBS TV documentary, *The Orwell Century*, broadcast in October 2002; Chris Durlacher's *George Orwell: A Life in Pictures* (aired on June 14, 2003), which garnered the Grierson Award for Best Documentary and the International

Emmy for Best Arts Production; and a South Bank TV special on Orwell (broadcast in July 2003), which was hosted by Orwell's newest biographer, D. J. Taylor.

The array of commemorative events was diverse. Among the highlights: Room 101 was recreated in 2003 at the Victoria & Albert Museum. (Disappointingly, it bore little relation to the BBC original of Orwell's day.) In May 2005, Lorin Maazel's opera, *Nineteen Eighty-Four* (with libretto by J. D. McClatchy and Thomas Meehan), opened at the Royal Opera House in Covent Garden.

Academic and literary interest in Orwell accelerated with the approach of 2003 and did not suddenly evaporate after June 25. Jeffrey Meyers published *Orwell: Wintry Conscience of a Generation* (2000), a biography that made extensive, intelligent use of Davison's path-breaking scholarship. New biographies by Gordon Bowker, *Inside George Orwell*, and by D. J. Taylor, *Orwell*, appeared; so did a short biography by Scott Lucas, *Orwell*. That year Lucas also published a severe critical study, *George Orwell and the Betrayal of Dissent*; and John Rodden's *Scenes from An Afterlife: The Legacy of George Orwell* appeared. Doubtless the scholarly extravaganza of the year was the international conference on Orwell held in May 2003 at Wellesley College in Massachusetts, which was attended by hundreds of Orwell's avid readers and at which two dozen prominent intellectuals and leading Orwell scholars spoke.

In 2004, Emma Larkin published an absorbing and engaging journey through contemporary Burma, *Secret Histories: Finding George Orwell in a Burmese Teashop*; and Rodden, along with Thomas Cushman, edited the proceedings of the 2003 centenary conference at Wellesley College, which they titled *George Orwell: Into the Twenty-First Century*. Not content to rest after the prodigious labor of his edition of *The Complete Works of George Orwell* (in twenty volumes), which was completed in 1999, Peter Davison published a supplementary volume, *The Lost Orwell* (2006); months later, Jean-Michel Place of Paris reproduced the Orwell–Raimbault correspondence in French translation in *George Orwell correspondence avec son traducteur René-Noël Raimbault*.[57]

Meanwhile, Dione Venables published a new edition of Jacintha Buddicom's *Eric & Us* in 2006. (It led to her hatching an innovative venture, the Orwell Forum website, in late 2007.) Soon thereafter, Dan Leab published *Orwell Subverted: The CIA and the Filming of Animal Farm* (2007) and John Rodden's edition of *The Cambridge Companion to George Orwell* (2007) appeared. Loraine Saunders revalued Orwell's early novels sharply upward in *The Unsung Artistry of George Orwell* (2008); and *Coming Up for Air* was performed as a dramatic monologue with considerable success (by Hal Cruttenden) at the Edinburgh Festival in 2008.

In the second decade of the twenty-first century, scholarly studies of Orwell and media attention to "Orwell" continue apace. This checklist merely covers a modest portion of the English-language work. For instance, dozens of scholarly articles and books were also published in German, Spanish, Polish, and even Japanese.

Representative anecdotes of Orwell's enduring celebrity status in the new millennium abound. One example was his appearance near the top of *Time* magazine's "Pop Chart" in August 2008. The occasion was that Orwell's diaries were being published in the blogosphere on a daily basis. A photograph of Orwell at the BBC sticks out among profiles of Brad Pitt, Britney Spears, Matthew McConaughey, Barack Obama, Clay Aiken's baby, a piece of Elvis memorabilia, and "the Crazy Puppy-Cloning Lady said to be a crazy 1970s sex fugitive." Under the image of its posthumous literary pop star, *Time* offered some sage counsel to the publishing industry: "Somebody get this guy a book deal!"[58]

A more recent instance is Orwell's presence in the "End-of-Year Quiz" for 2009 sponsored by *The Week*. Following color photos of Woody Allen, Nora Ephron, J. K. Rowling, and John Stewart, a black and white head shot of Orwell occupies the last frame of the page layout. "Whose Wit & Wisdom?" asks the subhead, challenging readers to identify the author of the selected quotations. (Unsurprisingly, Orwell's statement stands out for its old-fashioned seriousness: "If liberty means anything at all, it means the right to tell people what they do not want to hear.")[59]

Still another example, perhaps more ominously, was the news in October 2009 received by hundreds of Amazon Kindle owners, who awoke to discover that books by a certain famous author had mysteriously disappeared from their e-book readers. These were books that they had bought and paid for – and thought they owned. But no, apparently Orwell's publishing house changed its mind about offering an electronic edition, and Amazon, whose business lives and dies by publisher happiness, caved in. It electronically deleted Orwell's books from the Kindles and credited owners' accounts for the price. Wrote one outraged blogger:

> This is ugly for all kinds of reasons. Amazon says that this sort of thing is "rare," but that it can happen at all is unsettling; we've been taught to believe that e-books are, you know, just like books, only better. Already, we've learned that they're not really like books, in that once we're finished reading them, we can't resell or even donate them. But now we learn that all sales may not even be final.
>
> As one of my readers noted, it's like Barnes & Noble sneaking into our homes in the middle of the night, taking some books that we've been reading off our nightstands, and leaving us a check on the coffee table.

> You want to know the best part? The juicy, plump, dripping irony? The author who was the victim of this Big Brotherish plot was none other than George Orwell. And the books were *Nineteen Eighty-Four* and *Animal Farm*. Scary.[60]

Confronted by an incident with similarly ironic implications involving their famous former neighbor, residents of Hampstead did a better job than Amazon Books. During Rodden's 2009 visit with Ian Angus, who edited *CEJL* (with Sonia Orwell) in the 1960s, literary Hampstead was up in arms after a commemorative frieze of Orwell's face was stolen from a wall marking the location of Booklover's Corner, the second-hand shop where he worked in the 1930s. The criminal was not caught as no one saw who did it. A London journalist commented that he and most Hampstead denizens would advocate the installation of closed-circuit cameras at Booklover's Corner in the future – if that were not in such apparent violation of the convictions of the author of *Nineteen Eighty-Four*.

## An afterlife nonpareil

As Orwell's reputation entered the twenty-first century, he was recognized as the most widely read, serious English-language writer and most frequently cited political journalist of the twentieth century, with more than 60 million copies of his books published in sixty-two languages. *Animal Farm* and *Nineteen Eighty-Four* alone have sold more than 50 million copies, making them the bestselling pair of books by any author in history. Orwell had also become, in his famous phrase of Dickens, "a writer well worth stealing," and intellectuals on both the right and the left vied to be associated with him. Indeed they regularly moved his coffin in their direction. Without exaggeration, it could be said that Orwell and "Orwell" – the latter being the ideological totem and historical talisman – are today securely part of the political lexicon and cultural imagination of the West.

If Scott Fitzgerald claimed that "there are no second acts" in literature, Orwell has proven a great exception to that rule. His is indeed an afterlife nonpareil. A signal instance of Orwell's ongoing intellectual and cultural vitality is the collection of essays gathered from a 1999 symposium held at the University of Chicago. Edited by Abbott Gleason, Jack Goldsmith, and Martha Nussbaum, the volume announces itself as an attempt to gain an "unbiased and fresh perspective on Orwell's work by explicitly avoiding to include any contributions from established scholars of Orwell's life and work."

Is this not an utterly extraordinary statement to justify the publication of a scholarly work? Who else but Orwell would invite a book from which the keenest students of his work would be barred from appearing? Indeed, of what other literary figure could it possibly be said that a book from a major publisher such as Princeton University Press would appear in 2005 on the condition that no Orwell scholars are invited to contribute?

The editors' statement, proclaimed on the back cover of *On Nineteen Eighty-Four: Orwell and Our Future*, reflects not only Orwell's stature across many scholarly fields and academic disciplines, but also the irresistible urge among academic intellectuals to claim him for their own enterprises – or rather to deny, whether explicitly or implicitly, the claims of other scholars and domains of intellectual terrain any claim to him.

That a leading academic institution such as the University of Chicago bestowed their imprimatur on such a project says much about the "Orwell industry" and about the elitism of much contemporary cultural criticism. Orwell is, as it were, valuable intellectual property – to which this Orwell collection, whose contributors are chiefly lawyers and political scientists, testifies:

> This volume, like the conference, is not an exercise in Orwell criticism. Indeed, we quite deliberately did not include recognized Orwell scholars, and we did not seek standard literary interpretations of the novel. Instead, we asked a wide-ranging group of writers, all with their own agendas in social science, law, and the humanities, to give their own take on the novel, telling a general audience what it does offer us as we try to think about our future.[61]

This "deliberate" avoidance of recognized Orwell scholars did not preclude the contributors to the volume from drawing on Rodden's work and that of numerous other Orwell critics.

## "If Orwell were alive today …"

"Milton! thou shouldst be living at this hour: / England hath need of thee!" sighed Wordsworth in "London, 1802." Wordsworth cries out to the dead poet, John Milton, telling him that he should be alive, because England needs him now, because England has stagnated, its people selfish and unhappy, its splendor and power lost. But Milton could "raise us up, return to us again; / And give us manners, virtue, freedom, power."

Having recently passed (in 2008) the four-hundredth anniversary of Milton's death, one can lament that few living Englishmen (let alone others) would voice Wordsworth's sentiments. But consider this substitution: "Orwell! thou shouldst be living at this hour! England [and the world] hath need of thee!" *That* formulation is not so far-fetched at all. Indeed, it sums up the wish of so many readers to have Orwell on their side, the wistful musing "If Orwell were alive today."

Even though the question "If Orwell were alive today" is impossible to answer, the social psychology that drives us to ask this question recurrently is quite understandable. To that extent, it is legitimate to probe judiciously for how a posthumous figure like Orwell might assist us in the present. All kinds of people have been robbing his grave and quoting him out of context, almost as if his writings are sacred scripture. Obviously, the question as to what Orwell would say if he were alive today is on its face absurd. But people have wished strongly that Orwell were still alive today because he was the last intellectual who commanded full respect across the ideological spectrum from left to right. It would be possible to develop a fascinating study exclusively around the reverie, "If Orwell were alive today." Orwell's afterlife is so vital and present that he is more "alive" than countless persons who are still living, let alone many of his contemporaries who survived decades longer than he did into the latter half of the twentieth century.

Orwell's early death helped turn him into an icon endlessly claimed by the right and the left: "If Orwell were alive today" was actually the headline for a cover story penned by Norman Podhoretz, editor of *Commentary*, in 1984. He and others on the right, such as Irving Kristol, claimed Orwell as one of their own. Meanwhile, those who insisted that Orwell had affirmed that he was a democratic socialist to the end of his life argued that he would have agreed with them if he were alive today. So Orwell became a kind of deity for the secular intelligentsia, who began quoting him to their purpose. The argument from authority: who better suited for it than "Orwell," this twentieth-century "Saint George"?

Here we also arrive at a bizarre paradox. George Orwell has been celebrated by intellectuals and writers for a beautiful, pure, clean writing style: he is the "prose laureate" of modern English literature. Yet the essayist who in "Why I Write" aimed "to turn political writing into an art" and said that "Good prose is like a window pane" is the same author who coined the Newspeak words: "Big Brother Is Watching You," doublethink, thoughtcrime, Hate Week, and so on.

So Orwell is a doppelgänger. We have George Orwell, the champion of good prose and literary authenticity. But there is also "Orwellian," his very name as a proper adjective, which does not refer to the life he led or to good writing, but rather is a synonym for words such as oppressive, tyrannical, nightmarish, horrific: "Orwellian" state, "Orwellian" government, "Orwellian" language. Such doubleness has generated confusion and controversy – and has served to elevate his reputation.

The "saintly" reputation owes to the perceived life of the man and to his plain-man persona. Orwell became a figure who was perceived to live what he wrote and to have written from the depth of his experiences. Unlike so many other writers and intellectuals of his day, he didn't simply observe a phenomenon and then pen a column, short story, or novel about it. Instead he went there, he experienced it, and he wrote about it out of the depths of his experiences. Orwell went to live with the down and outs in London and Paris. Three years later, when the miners in the north of England were suffering in what was still the depths of the Depression, he took a trip to the north and from it emerged *The Road to Wigan Pier*. A few months later, when civil war in Spain broke out, Orwell went to fight against the fascists, not to simply lounge in hotels and send cable reports back home like other intellectuals of his generation. It was this intimate connection between the life he led and the work he wrote that so inspired many people, assisted by clear, transparent writing. His living voice within the work represented a connection between the man and the work that others valued. One can still hear Orwell's living voice today.

By contrast, when used as an *ad hominem* attack, Orwell's name in adjectival form represents a kind of Newspeak itself. The use of "Orwellian" is, as it were, *doubleplusungood*. One example of how Orwell's coinages become "*doubleplusungood*" is the attitude of the Austin, Texas, police chief in a November 2009 speech to the city's Rotary Club. Chief Art Acevedo urged that new funding be provided to utilize state-of-the-art technology to prevent crime. Acevedo declared: "Big Brothers are actually good, they keep an eye out for you." Nonetheless, he voiced support for Austin's beloved slogan: "If we need to Keep Austin Weird, we can, but we need to stop keeping safety weird."[62]

## A reputation evergreen

As we proceed through the second decade of the twenty-first century, therefore, Orwell is merely dead chronologically. That is, in terms of his historical and ongoing impact, he is still quite alive today. Why? Because *Nineteen Eighty-Four* failed as a prophecy and succeeded as a warning. *Nineteen Eighty-Four* is not just a work of science fiction, nor is it simply a political critique of Stalinism, or Nazism, or both rolled in as one as totalitarianism. That is to say, *Nineteen Eighty-Four* led to 1989, it led to the collapse of the Soviet empire and the breakup of the Eastern European bloc. Insofar as any book, or any idea, can be said to have had a direct impact on political affairs, *Nineteen Eighty-Four* did.

As an admonition to the intellectuals and the policymakers in the early postwar era, *Nineteen Eighty-Four* exerted decisive influence. Because *Nineteen Eighty-Four* was such a powerful warning, it succeeded in changing the tide of public opinion. Orwell became the most famous literary Cold Warrior. His reputation and the relevance of the book are not, however, limited to the Cold War. The Union of Soviet *Socialist* Republics is no more, and National *Socialism* is no more – and Orwell's book was indeed to a great extent a broadside against such abuses of "socialism" – but the pertinence of Orwell's work is not restricted to the wartime and Cold War eras. Otherwise *Nineteen Eighty-Four* would be a book just about the past – after all, the quarter-century anniversary of 1984 passed by in 2009.

Yet *Nineteen Eighty-Four* is not just about Nazism, or Stalinism, or communism, or any of their variants; it is also about the abuse of language: its bowdlerization, its manipulation, its corruption. It is also about the invasion of privacy, and all of the insidious technologies that have been invented that rape our souls and impoverish our minds. It is also about all kinds of technical gadgetry that, while seeming to have such promise, eventually can undermine and rob us of our spirit. It is also about the little "big brothers." If indeed there are no Stalins, no Hitlers on the world scene, there are nonetheless the rogue states, the corrupt dictators such as Robert Mugabe, Kim Jong-il in North Korea, and the Castro brothers in Cuba. Just because there are no Big Brothers does not mean no less evil "little brothers" do not still reign.

In this connection, we can venture one prophecy about Orwell. If he had lived, Orwell would be targeting such tyrants as examples of leaders corrupted by power. Two of his greatest concerns were indeed the servile state and the danger of leader worship. Insofar as this young century continues to witness many of the abuses that he pointed out in *Animal Farm* and *Nineteen Eighty-Four*, he and his work continue to be relevant. And so long as those abuses – ranging from the corruptions of language and the abuses of technology to the invasions of privacy and the evils of authoritarianism – can easily morph in a totalitarian direction, *Nineteen Eighty-Four* and Orwell continue to be pertinent in our time.

The debates about Orwell – and "Orwell" – will continue so long as this relevance endures. As they do, so too will the speculations about Orwell's stances and positions on contemporary events. Readers will continue to wonder: if Orwell were alive today, if he had come to see that it wasn't just the first example of state socialism – Stalinism in the USSR – that ran around in pig's clothing, if it wasn't just this early corrupt form of socialism, if all of the successor states that called themselves "socialist" and "communist" had turned out to develop forms of economic and political collectivism that also led to tyranny, could he possibly have remained a socialist? Or might he have seen, a half-century or more later, that history has taught us this: when power is concentrated into hands that are centralized in a collectivist fashion economically, politically and otherwise, when pigs rule, what will inexorably occur is oppression and tyranny. Might he have turned against socialism itself?

The question is fair. One reason Orwell wrote such a supportive review of Friedrich Hayek's *The Road to Serfdom* was that he sensed that socialism might inevitably lead to "the servile state" which Hilaire Belloc warned against, i.e., eventually to totalitarianism. Arguably, that lesson was still too early to be drawn in 1950. Other state socialisms were on the horizon. Orwell himself still hoped that his own brand of socialism – such as when he fought in Spain for the Loyalists against Franco – might indeed come to power, that is, a socialism that would mean justice and liberty for all.

Orwell was a socialist because of his experience, not because of some kind of an abstract intellectual formula. That is to say, he was a *socialist*, but he was not a *progressive*. He was against the injustices and the lack of freedom that he saw under state capitalism. But if he had seen that these post-Stalinist forms of state socialism had also led to oligarchical collectivism, might he not have repudiated socialism as an economic and political system? Yes, the question is justified and compelling.

Looking back from the present, it is clear that the decade immediately following Orwell's death constituted the crucial period in the making (and partial freezing) of his reputation. The oft-quoted critical commonplaces (and myths) about Orwell the man, the entry of Newspeak into the political lexicon, the introduction of his work into school curricula, the mass media adaptations of *Animal Farm* and *Nineteen Eighty-Four*, the political abuses of Orwell's name and work: all of these developments were well under way by the late 1950s. They are among the main causes and consequences of Orwell's monumental public status.

Today Orwell enjoys a public literary reputation that has no rival among contemporary authors – a reputation that, in fact, has had virtually no peer among writers for decades. Indeed, Orwell could well describe his afterlife by borrowing Horace's smug, self-glorifying summation of his own achievement in *Ode XXX*:

> More durable than bronze, higher than Pharoah's
> Pyramids is the monument I have made,
> A shape that angry wind or hungry rain
> Cannot demolish, nor the innumerable
> Ranks of the years that march in centuries.

I shall not wholly die: some part of me
Will cheat the goddess of death, for while High Priest
And Vestal shall climb our Capital in a hush,
My reputation grass shall keep green and growing.

Whether the prophecy in that last line will continue to be borne out by history in Orwell's case is uncertain. *Non omnis moriar:* "I shall not wholly die." But will that still be true of Orwell a century hence – let alone another two millennia? It is doubtful.

Non omnis mortuus est. "Not all of him has died." Yet if Orwell remains "alive" and present, it is not only because the world has not passed him by, but also because the writer spoke in a voice so plain and so insistent that he has continued to command the world's attention. Not only the age which has received Orwell, then, but also the literary achievement which has helped shape it account for his remaining "a figure in our lives." And so also do observers' discrepant perceptions of the adamantly unsainted man, so fiercely hated and so dearly loved.[63]

More than six decades after his death, however, the heated political battles for Orwell's mantle still simmer. But with the passing of milestones such as 1984 and 2003, Orwell's reputation has now entered a new phase. Perhaps it will compare with the relative ideological calm and scholarly turn of the late 1980s and early 1990s. Or with the period of the late 1950s and early 1960s, during which his overall reputation dipped because of a perception that the Orwell industry had overheated and that critical and popular interest in "Orwell" had reached the saturation point. But this latter scenario seems improbable. It is more likely that Orwell and "Orwell" will continue to engage both the general public, even if on a much lower scale than during 2002–3. Scholarly interest will doubtless remain high. Spurred by the publication of Davison's edition of *The Complete Works of George Orwell*, academic attention may shift decisively from "Orwell" to Orwell's non-fiction and life, a trend that the biographies of 2000–3 anticipated.

The foregoing reflections do not account fully for the "afterlives" of "Orwell." But they do illuminate how the writer George Orwell has metamorphosed into "the Orwell legend." Indeed, they take his "afterlife and times" beyond both the "Orwell century" and the Orwell centenary, letting us behold, as Malcolm Muggeridge once wrote about his friend, "how the legend of a human being is created."

# Notes

## Introduction

1. Sonia Orwell and Ian Angus (eds.), *The Collected Essays, Journalism and Letters of George Orwell* (New York: Harcourt, Brace, and World, 1968; hereafter cited as *CEJL*), IV, 515.
2. *CEJL*, I, 1.
3. Ibid., 6.
4. Ibid., 3.
5. Michael Shelden, *Orwell: The Authorized Biography* (New York: HarperCollins, 1991), 3.
6. *CEJL*, I, 7.
7. "Politics and the English Language," *CEJL*, IV, 137.
8. Bernard Crick, *George Orwell: A Life* (Boston: Little, Brown, and Co., 1980), 22.
9. George Orwell, *Down and Out in Paris and London* (Harmondsworth: Penguin, 1971), 113.
10. Peter Davison (ed.), *The Complete Works of George Orwell*, 20 vols. (London: Secker & Warburg, 1999), XVI, essay on Arthur Koestler, 2548.
11. George Orwell, "My Country Right or Left,"*CEJL*, I, 539.
12. Ibid.
13. Letter to John Middleton Murry, August 5, 1944, *CEJL*, III, 203.
14. *Nineteen Eighty-Four* (New York: New American Library, Signet Classic, 1987), 220.

## 1 Life and context

1. Crick, *Orwell*, 53.
2. See for example, Daphne Patai, *The Orwell Mystique: A Study in Male Ideology* (Amherst: University of Massachusetts Press, 1984).
3. Crick, *Orwell*, 89.
4. Gordon Bowker, *Inside George Orwell: A Biography* (London: Palgrave Macmillan, 2003), 188.
5. Ibid., 21–22.
6. Crick, *Orwell*, Appendix B, 586–89.
7. Shelden, *Orwell*, 80.

8. Bowker, *Inside George Orwell*, 70.
9. Shelden, *Orwell*, 97.
10. For Orwell's anger at his time in the service of the British Empire see Part II of *The Road to Wigan Pier*.
11. Stephen Ingle, "The Anti-Imperialism of George Orwell," in Graham Holderness, Bryan Loughrey, and Nahem Yousaf (eds.), *George Orwell: Contemporary Critical Essays* (New York: St. Martins Press, 1998), 230.
12. Shelden, *Orwell*, 115.
13. Bowker, *Inside George Orwell*, 141.
14. *Down and Out*, 113.
15. Michael Levenson, "The Fictional Realist: The Novels of the 1930s," in John Rodden (ed.), *The Cambridge Companion to George Orwell* (Cambridge University Press, 2007), 66.
16. Crick, *Orwell*, 34.
17. *CEJL*, I, 224.
18. Shelden, *Orwell*, 152.
19. Ibid., 172.
20. Crick, *Orwell*, 248.
21. *CEJL*, I, 153.
22. Ibid., 224.
23. *The Road to Wigan Pier* (San Diego: Harvest HBJ Book, 1958), 15.
24. Dwight Macdonald, *Discriminations: Essays and Afterthoughts, 1938–1974* (New York: Viking Press, 1974), 320–24.
25. *CEJL*, I, 256.
26. Crick, *Orwell*, 254.
27. Bowker, *Inside George Orwell*, 199.
28. Malcolm Muggeridge, "A Knight of Woeful Countenance," in Miriam Gross (ed.), *The World of George Orwell* (New York: Simon & Schuster, 1972).
29. *CEJL*, I, 268–69.
30. Bowker, *Inside George Orwell*, 247.
31. Crick, *Orwell*, 294–95.
32. *CEJL*, I, 539.
33. Ibid., 493–527.
34. *CEJL*, II, 340.
35. Ibid., 56–109.
36. Ibid., II, 286.
37. Jeffrey Meyers, *Orwell: The Wintry Conscience of a Generation* (New York: W. W. Norton, 2000), 251.

## 2 Works

1. *CEJL*, I, 3–7.
2. *CEJL*, II, 23–24.

3. Loraine Saunders, *The Unsung Artistry of George Orwell: The Novels From Burmese Days to Nineteen Eighty-Four* (Aldershot: Ashgate, 2008).
4. Meyers, *Wintry Conscience*, 325.
5. See *The Road to Wigan Pier*, chapter 9.
6. Shelden, *Orwell*, 176.
7. David Smith and Michael Mosher, *Orwell for Beginners* (London: Writers and Readers, 1984), 69.
8. Peter Davison, *Orwell: A Literary Life* (New York: Palgrave, 1996), 47.
9. Ibid., 49.
10. Bowker, *Inside George Orwell*, 148.
11. Shelden, *Orwell*, 179–80.
12. Patai, *Mystique*, 97.
13. Shelden, *Orwell*, 190.
14. Ibid., 206.
15. Patai, *Mystique*, 97.
16. Davison, *Orwell*, 58–62.
17. Crick, *Orwell*, 257.
18. Patai, *Mystique*, 110.
19. George Orwell, *Keep the Aspidistra Flying* (London: Secker & Warburg, 1954), 303.
20. D. J. Taylor, *Orwell: The Life* (New York: Henry Holt & Company, 2003), 173.
21. Bowker, *Inside George Orwell*, 428.
22. Ibid., 239.
23. Crick, *Orwell*, 368.
24. Meyers, *Wintry Conscience*, 190.
25. George Orwell, *Coming Up for Air* (London: Secker & Warburg, 1963), 172.
26. Ibid., 160.
27. Saunders, *Unsung Artistry*, 22.
28. Ibid., 23.
29. *CEJL*, I, 19.
30. Quoted in Bowker, *Inside George Orwell*, 132.
31. Orwell, *Down and Out*, 5.
32. Ibid., 6.
33. Crick, *Orwell*, 214.
34. Orwell, *Down and Out*, 121.
35. Ibid., 189.
36. Orwell, *Road to Wigan Pier*, 5.
37. Ibid., 8.
38. Ibid., 12.
39. Ibid., 18.
40. Ibid., 23.
41. Ibid., 189.
42. Ibid., 174.
43. Shelden, *Orwell*, 230.

44. George Orwell, *Homage to Catalonia* (Boston: Beacon Press, 1955), 5.
45. George Orwell, "Looking Back on the Spanish War," *CEJL*, II, 254.
46. Ibid., 97.
47. Ibid.
48. George Orwell, "Spilling the Spanish Beans," *CEJL*, I, 270.
49. George Orwell, "Why I Write," *CEJL*, I, 5.
50. Orwell, "Looking Back on the Spanish War," *CEJL*, II, 266–67.
51. *CEJL*, I, 535.
52. *CEJL*, II, 13–15.
53. *CEJL*, I, 242–47.
54. Bowker, *Inside George Orwell*, 88–89; Shelden, *Orwell*, 102.
55. *Road to Wigan Pier*, 146.
56. "A Hanging," *CEJL*, I, 45.
57. Ibid., 45.
58. Ibid., I, 44–49.
59. "Shooting an Elephant," *CEJL*, I, 235.
60. Ibid., 238.
61. Davison, *Orwell*, 47.
62. *CEJL*, I, 235–47.
63. Davison, *Orwell*, 147.
64. "Charles Dickens," *CEJL*, I, 460.
65. "Inside the Whale," *CEJL*, I, 526.
66. Ibid.
67. Bowker, *Inside George Orwell*, 346.
68. Patai, *Mystique*, 147.
69. Shelden, *Orwell*, 431.
70. Philip Bounds, *Orwell and Marxism: The Political and Cultural Thinking of George Orwell* (London and New York: I. B. Tauris, 2009), 71.
71. *CEJL*, IV, 139.
72. *The Lion and the Unicorn*, *CEJL*, II, 56.
73. Miriam Gross (ed.), *The World of George Orwell* (New York: Simon & Schuster, 1972), 114–15.
74. Preface to the Ukrainian edition of *Animal Farm*, *CEJL*, III, 405–6.
75. Davison, *Orwell*, 9.
76. Shelden, *Orwell*, 371.
77. Peter Davison (ed.), *Orwell: A Life in Letters* (London: Harvill Secker, 2010), 512; *CEJL*, IV, 131.
78. *CEJL*, III, 95.
79. "Why I Write," *CEJL*, I, 1–7.
80. John Newsinger, *Orwell's Politics* (Basingstoke: Palgrave Macmillan, 2002), 118.
81. Review of *Russia under Soviet Rule* by N. de Basily, *CEJL*, I, 381.
82. Taylor, *Orwell*, 334.
83. Ibid., 334.

84. Ibid., 333.
85. Crick, *Orwell*, 461.
86. Ibid., 455–56.
87. Meyers, *Wintry Conscience*, 246.
88. Peter Davison (ed.), *The Lost Orwell: The Lost Letters and Writings of George Orwell* (London: Timewell Press, 2006), 148–49.
89. Shelden, *Orwell*, 368.
90. Martin Stannard, *Evelyn Waugh: The Later Years, 1939–1965* (London: Norton & Co., 1992), 165, note 81.
91. Meyers, *Wintry Conscience*, 251.
92. Shelden, *Orwell*, 371.
93. "Why I Write," *CEJL*, I, 7.
94. Bowker, *Inside George Orwell*, 371.
95. Davison, *Literary Life*, 103–4.
96. *Nineteen Eighty-Four*, 224.
97. Patai, *Mystique*, 15.
98. John Newsinger, *Orwell's Politics* (Basingstoke: Palgrave Macmillan, 2002), 105.
99. Davison (ed.), *Life in Letters*, 452.
100. Ibid., 459.
101. Crick, *Orwell*, 569.
102. Irving Howe, *Politics and the Novel* (Chicago: Ivan R. Dee, 2002), 240.

## 3 Critical reception

1. *Times Literary Supplement,* January 12, 1933, 22.
2. *Adelphi*, February 1933, 382.
3. *New Statesman and Nation*, March 18, 1933, 338.
4. *Nation*, September 6, 1933, 279.
5. *Adelphi*, August 1935, 316–17.
6. *New Statesman and Nation*, April 25, 1936, 635,
7. *New Statesman and Nation*, March 23, 1935, 422.
8. *Observer*, March 10, 1935, 6.
9. *Spectator*, March 22, 1935, 504.
10. *Adelphi*, June 1936, 190.
11. *Time and Tide*, March 20, 1937, 382.
12. *Fortnightly*, April 1937, 505–6.
13. *Daily Worker*, March 17, 1937.
14. *CEJL*, I, 269.
15. *New Leader*, May 6, 1937, 7.
16. *New English Weekly*, May 26, 1937, 129–30.
17. *Time and Tide*, April 10, 1938, 599–600.
18. Lionel Trilling, Introduction to *Homage to Catalonia* (Boston: Beacon Press, 1952), vii.

19. *Times Literary Supplement*, June 17, 1939, 355.
20. *Tribune*, July 21, 1939, 11.
21. *Time and Tide*, March 9, 1940, 257–8.
22. *New English Weekly*, March 14, 1940, 307–8.
23. *Times Literary Supplement*, April 20, 1940, 192.
24. *Adelphi*, April 1940, 316–17.
25. *Scrutiny*, September 1940, 173–76.
26. *Listener*, March 6, 1941, 349.
27. *New Statesmen and Nation*, March 1, 1941, 216.
28. *Partisan Review*, March 1942, 166–69.
29. *Spectator*, August 17, 1945, 156.
30. *Horizon*, September 1945, 215–16.
31. *New Statesman and Nation*, September 8, 1945, 165–66.
32. *The Tablet*, April 6, 1946, 176.
33. Quoted in Bowker, *Inside George Orwell*, 345.
34. *Spectator*, March 8, 1946, 250–52.
35. *Saturday Review of Literature*, May 11, 1946, 11.
36. *Partisan Review*, September 1946, 500–4.
37. *New Statesman and Nation*, February 16, 1946, 124.
38. *Partisan Review*, July 1949, 743–49.
39. *Reynolds News*, June 12, 1949, 4.
40. I. Anisimov, "Enemies of Mankind," *Pravda*, May 12, 1950.
41. Arthur Koestler, *The Trail of the Dinosaur* (London: Vintage, 1994), 47–48.
42. *World Review*, June 16, 1950, 51.
43. *New Statesman and Nation*, January 28, 1950, 96.
44. *World Review*, June 1950, 5–7.
45. *Listener*, November 2, 1950, 471.
46. *Kenyon Review*, Winter 1954, 139–44.
47. Raymond Williams, *Politics and Letters* (London: Verso, 1981), 384.
48. *Esquire*, March 1969, 12–14.
49. *Daily Telegraph*, October 3, 1968, 22.
50. *Harper's*, January 1969, 97.
51. John Rodden, *The Politics of Literary Reputation: The Making and Claiming of "St. George" Orwell* (Oxford University Press, 1989), 321.
52. *Listener*, December 12, 1968, 797–98.
53. *New Yorker*, March 1969, 139–51.
54. Quoted in Alvin Kernan, *In Plato's Cave* (New Haven: Yale University Press, 1999), 13.
55. Victor Troppi, "1984: Full Circle," *New Times*, December 1983, 22–24.
56. On the concept of "volcanic" moments in reputation-building, see Rodden, *The Politics of Literary Reputation*, 272, 419.
57. I am grateful to Peter Davison for alerting me to several of the Orwell events that occurred during 2002–6.

58. "Pop Chart," *Time*, August 25, 2008, 19.

59. *The Week*, December 25, 2009/January 8, 2010, 27.

60. David Pogue, "Some E-Books Are More Equal Than Others," July 17, 2009, pogue. blogs.nytimes.com.

61. Martha Nussbaum, Abbott Gleason, and Jack Goldsmith (eds.), *On Nineteen Eighty-Four: Orwell and Our Future* (Princeton University Press, 2005), back cover.

62. *Daily Texan*, Austin, Texas, November 25, 2009, 6.

63. Rodden, *The Politics of Literary Reputation*, 321.

# Select bibliography

## Primary works

### George Orwell's major works

*Down and Out in Paris and London* (1933)
*Burmese Days* (1934)
*A Clergyman's Daughter* (1935)
*Keep the Aspidistra Flying* (1936)
*The Road to Wigan Pier* (1937)
*Homage to Catalonia* (1938)
*Coming Up for Air* (1939)
*Inside the Whale* (1940)
*The Lion and the Unicorn* (1941)
*Animal Farm* (1945)
*Critical Essays* (1945; American title: *Dickens, Dali and Others* 1946)
*Nineteen Eighty-Four* (1949)

### Editions

*The Collected Essays, Journalism and Letters of George Orwell*, ed. Sonia Orwell and
        Ian Angus, 4 volumes. New York: Harcourt, Brace, and World, 1968
*The Complete Works of George Orwell*, ed. Peter Davison, 20 volumes. London:
        Secker & Warburg, 1999.
*The Diaries of George Orwell*, ed. Peter Davison. London: Harvill Secker, 2009.
*The Lost Orwell: The Lost Letters and Writings of George Orwell*, ed. Peter Davison.
        London: Timewell Press, 2006.
*Nineteen Eighty-Four: The Facsimile of the Extant Manuscript*, ed. Peter Davison.
        San Diego: Harcourt, Brace, Jovanovich, 1984.

## Secondary sources

Anisimov, I. "Enemies of Mankind," *Pravda*, May 12, 1950.
Atkins, John. *George Orwell: A Literary Study*. London: Calder and Zoyars 1954.
Bounds, Philip. *Orwell and Marxism: The Political and Cultural Thinking of
        George Orwell*. London and New York: I. B. Tauris, 2009.

Bowker, Gordon. *Inside George Orwell*. London: Palgrave Macmillan, 2003.

Brander, Lawrence. *George Orwell*. London: Longman's, Green & Co., 1954.

Brunsdale, Mitzi. *Student Companion to George Orwell*. Westport, CT: Greenwood Press. 2000.

Buddicom, Jacintha, *Eric & Us*. The Postscript Edition. London: Finlay, 2006.

Connolly, Cyril. *Enemies of Promise*. New York: Garden City, 1960.

Crick, Bernard. *George Orwell: A Life*. Boston: Little, Brown, and Co. 1980. Revised edition, 1992.

Crick, Bernard and Coppard, Audrey. *Orwell Remembered*. New York: Facts on File, 1984.

Cushman, Thomas and Rodden, John. *George Orwell: Into the Twenty-First Century*. Boulder, CO: Paradigm Press, 2004.

Davison, Peter. *George Orwell: A Literary Life*. New York: Palgrave, 1996.

Fyvel, Tosco. *George Orwell: A Personal Memoir*. London: Macmillan, 1982.

Gottlieb, Erika. *The Orwell Conundrum: A Cry of Despair or Faith in the Spirit of Man*. Ottawa: Carleton University Press, 1992.

Gross, Miriam (ed.). *The World of George Orwell*. New York: Simon & Schuster, 1972.

Hitchens, Christopher, *Why Orwell Matters*. New York: Basic Books, 2002.

Holderness, Graham, Loughrey, Bryan and Yousaf, Nahem (eds.), *George Orwell: Contemporary Critical Essays*. New York St. Martins Press, 1998.

Hollis, Christopher. *A Study of George Orwell*. London: Hollis & Carter, 1956.

Hopkinson, Tom. *George Orwell*. London and New York: Longman's Grace & Co., 1953.

Howe, Irving. *Politics and the Novel,* Chicago: Ivan R. Dee, 2002.

(ed.). *Orwell's Nineteen Eighty-Four*. New York: Harcourt, Brace, Jovanovich, 1982.

Judt, S. "I Once Met George Orwell," in Richard Ingrams, (ed.), *I Once Met: Unexpected Encounters with the Famous and Infamous*. London: Oldie Publications, 2008.

Katz, Wendy. "Imperialism and Patriotism: Orwell's Dilemma in 1940," *Modernist Studies: Literature and Culture*, 3 (1979), 99–105.

Kogan, Steve. "In Celebration of George Orwell on the Fiftieth Anniversary of 'Politics and the English Language,'" *Academic Questions* (Winter 1996–97), 15–29.

Lebedoff, David. *The Same Man: George Orwell and Evelyn Waugh in Love and War*. New York: Random House, 2008.

Lucas, Scott. *Orwell*. London: Haus, 2003.

Lutman, Stephen. "Orwell's Patriotism," *Journal of Contemporary History*, 2/2 (1967), 149–58.

Meyers, Jeffrey. *George Orwell: The Critical Heritage*. New York: Routledge, 1997.

*Orwell: The Wintry Conscience of a Generation*. New York and London: W. W. Norton, 2000.

*A Reader's Guide to George Orwell*. New York: Littlefield, Adam, 1977.

Michéa, Jean-Claude. *Orwell, anarchiste Tory. Suivi de À propos de 1984*. Paris: Climats, 2008.

Newsinger, John. *Orwell's Politics*. Basingstoke: Palgrave Macmillan, 2002.

Patai, Daphne. *The Orwell Mystique: A Study in Male Ideology*. Amherst: University of Massachusetts Press, 1984.

Rees, Richard. *George Orwell: A Fugitive From the Camp of Justice*. Southern Illinois University Press, 1965.

Rodden, John. *Every Intellectual's Big Brother: George Orwell's Literary Siblings*. Austin: University of Texas Press, 2008.

   *The Politics of Literary Reputation: The Making and Claiming of "St. George" Orwell*. Oxford University Press, 1989.

   *Scenes from an Afterlife: The Legacy of George Orwell*. Wilmington, DE: ISI Books, 2003.

   *The Unexamined Orwell*. Austin: University of Texas Press, 2011.

   (ed.). *George Orwell: Critical Insights*. Ipswich, MA: Salon Press, 2012.

   (ed.). *The Cambridge Companion to George Orwell*. Cambridge University Press, 2007.

   (ed. with Thomas Cushman). *George Orwell: Into the Twenty-First Century*. Boulder: Paradigm Publishers, 2004.

   (ed.). *Understanding Animal Farm: A Student Casebook to Issues, Sources and Historical Documents*. Westport, CT: Greenwood Press, 1999.

Rose, Jonathan (ed.). *The Revised Orwell*. East Lansing: Michigan State University Press, 1992.

Saunders, Loraine. *The Unsung Artistry of George Orwell: The Novels from Burmese Days to Nineteen Eighty-Four*. Aldershot: Ashgate, 2008.

Shelden, Michael. *Orwell: The Authorized Biography*. New York: HarperCollins, 1991.

Smith, David and Mosher, Michael. *Orwell For Beginners*. London: Writers and Readers, 1984.

Spurling, Hillary. *The Girl From the Fiction Department*. London: Counterpoint, 2002.

Stansky, Peter and Abrahams, William. *Orwell: The Transformation*. New York: Knopf, 1980.

   *The Unknown Orwell*. Stanford University Press, 1972.

Symons, Julian. "Orwell: A Reminiscence." *London Magazine*, 3 (September 1963), 35–49.

Taylor, D. J. *Orwell: The Life*. London: Henry Holt, 2003.

Trilling, Lionel. Introduction to George Orwell's *Homage to Catalonia*. Boston: Beacon Press, 1952.

Troppi, Victor. "'1984': Full Circle," *New Times*, December 1983.

Tyrell, Martin. *The Politics of George Orwell (1903–1950): From Tory Anarchism to National Socialism and More Than Half Way Back*, Cultural Notes, 36. London: Libertarian Alliance, 1997

Wadhams, Stephen. *Remembering George Orwell*. London: Penguin, 1984.

Walter, N. *George Orwell: At Home and Amongst the Anarchists*. London: Freedom Press, 1998.

West, William J. *Orwell: The Lost Writings*. New York: Arbor House, 1985.

*Orwell: The War Commentaries*. New York: Pantheon, 1986.

Wilkin, P. *The Strange Case of Tory Anarchism*. London: Libri, 2010.

Williams, Raymond. *George Orwell*. Englewood Cliffs, NJ: Prentice-Hall, 1974.

Woodcock, George. *The Crystal Spirit*. Boston: Little, Brown, 1967.

Zwerdling, Alex. *Orwell and the Left*. New Haven: Yale University Press, 1974.

# Index

# Cambridge Introductions to…

**Authors**

*Margaret Atwood* Heidi Macpherson
*Jane Austen* Janet Todd
*Samuel Beckett* Ronan McDonald
*Walter Benjamin* David Ferris
*Chekhov* James N. Loehlin
*J. M. Coetzee* Dominic Head
*Samuel Taylor Coleridge* John Worthen
*Joseph Conrad* John Peters
*Jacques Derrida* Leslie Hill
*Charles Dickens* Jon Mee
*Emily Dickinson* Wendy Martin
*George Eliot* Nancy Henry
*T. S. Eliot* John Xiros Cooper
*William Faulkner* Theresa M. Towner
*F. Scott Fitzgerald* Kirk Curnutt
*Michel Foucault* Lisa Downing
*Robert Frost* Robert Faggen
*Gabriel Garcia Marquez* Gerald Martin
*Nathaniel Hawthorne* Leland S. Person
*Zora Neale Hurston* Lovalerie King
*James Joyce* Eric Bulson
*Thomas Mann* Todd Kontje
*Christopher Marlowe* Tom Rutter
*Herman Melville* Kevin J. Hayes
*Milton* Stephen B. Dobranski
*George Orwell* John Rodden and John Rossi
*Sylvia Plath* Jo Gill
*Edgar Allan Poe* Benjamin F. Fisher
*Ezra Pound* Ira Nadel
*Marcel Proust* Adam Watt
*Jean Rhys* Elaine Savory
*Edward Said* Conor McCarthy
*Shakespeare* Emma Smith
*Shakespeare's Comedies* Penny Gay
*Shakespeare's History Plays* Warren Chernaik
*Shakespeare's Poetry* Michael Schoenfeldt
*Shakespeare's Tragedies* Janette Dillon
*Harriet Beecher Stowe* Sarah Robbins
*Mark Twain* Peter Messent
*Edith Wharton* Pamela Knights
*Walt Whitman* M. Jimmie Killingsworth
*Virginia Woolf* Jane Goldman
*William Wordsworth* Emma Mason
*W. B. Yeats* David Holdeman

**Topics**